2 Cool Cards

Edited by
David E. Carter

...and I helped!
Suzanna
Brown

Cool Cards, Two

First published in 2000 by HBI,
an imprint of HarperCollins Publishers
10 East 53rd Street
New York, NY 10022-5299

Distributed in the U.S. and Canada by
Watson-Guptill Publications
1515 Broadway
New York, NY 10036
Tel: (800) 451-1741
              (732) 363-4511 in NJ, AK, HI
Fax: (732) 363-0338
Paperback ISBN: 0-8230-7478-1

Distributed throughout the rest of the world by
HarperCollins International
10 East 53rd Street
New York, NY 10022-5299
Fax: (212) 207-7654
Hardcover ISBN: 0688-17980-0

First published in Germany by Nippan
Nippon Shuppan Hanbai
Deutschland GmbH
Krefelder Strasse 85
D-40549 Dusseldorf
Tel: (0211) 5048089
Fax: (0211) 5049326
ISBN: 3-931884-62-7

Printed in Hong Kong by Everbest Printing Company through
Four Colour Imports, Louisville, Kentucky.

If you liked cool cards, then you'll love the sequel, **Cool Cards, Two**—coming soon to a theater near you!

No...wait. That's a movie intro. This is a **book**.

But, on second thought, the same thing applies (all but the part about coming to a theater near you). In fact, since you have the book in your hands, hopefully, it has a destiny at a cash register near you. But I digress.

Back to the book—the original cool cards was very popular since it showed a lot of really original non-corporate business cards from designers from a lot of places. We really believe that **Cool Cards, Two** will be similar to Godfather II—that is, it will be better than the original (without the violence, of course).

So, if you're pondering buying this book, remember the words, "I have an offer you can't refuse...buy this book."

David E. Carter

P.S.
No animals were harmed in the production of this book.

the creative firm of

**Peter Taflan Marketing
Communications, Inc.**
Durham, North Carolina
with real-life designer
Janssen Strother
created these business cards for
Linda Dickerson Interiors

One side of interior designer cards incorporate script and serif
fonts for text; opposite is printed with beautiful fabric swatches
which hint at the company's decorating style.

ĕm dash design:

Erika K. Maxwell
Art Director

Post Office Box 410
Richmond, Virginia 23218
☏ + 🖨 804·321·3801
emdashs@earthlink.net

the creative firm of
em dash design
Richmond, Virginia
with real-life designer
Erika K. Maxwell
created this business card for
em dash design

Interesting typography includes a narrow, serif E and a large, block, "rubber-stamped" M. Accent above the first letter in the design firm's name clues the readers into the correct pronunciation.

the creative firm of
Siebert Design
Dayton, Ohio
with real-life designer
Lori Siebert
created this business card for
Scott Hull Associates

This business card for an illustrator has a feeling of handwork, as opposed to computer rendering. Pencil-scrawled information offers no pretense while visually reiterating the claim, "I am what I am."

the creative firm of
Direction Design
Los Angeles, California
produced this business card
with real-life creative director & designer
Anja Mueller
and managing director
Teresa E. Lopez

Crop-marked and hand-cut window is a great visual
for a photographer's business card.

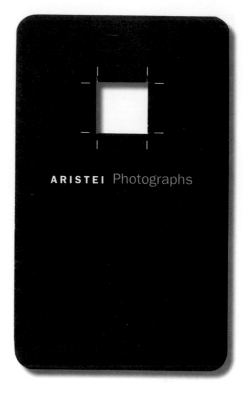

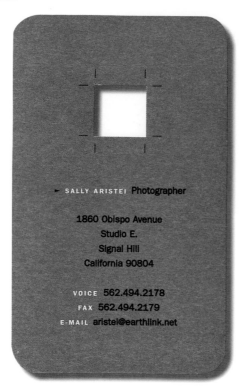

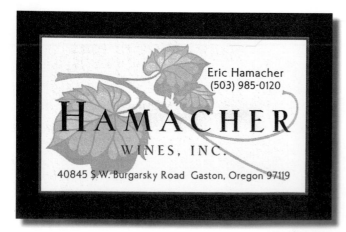

the creative firm of
Anstey Healy Design
Portland, Oregon
with real-life designers
**Abigail Anstey &
Catherine Healy**
created this business card for
Hamacher Wines

Two-color card for a wine company is printed in appropriate colors
of burgundy and dusty green. Name of business is embossed, as is
the green outline which separates the card's text from its border.

the creative firms of
Steve Trapero Design/
Print Media & Design, Inc.
Silver Spring, Maryland
with real-life designer
Steve Trapero
created this business card for
Metropolitan Consulting Corporation

The text treatment is the strength of this layout. Tall and thin, very
Art Deco, font in name logo is balanced by a wide and short card.

the creative firm of
Boldface Design
Hollywood, California
with real-life designers
Jeffrey Buice, Kevin Hummer
created this business card for
Melamed Management

With reference to this company's initials, a logo was created and
then blind embossed on the card. Certain numerals within the
address are given special treatment by differing point sizes.

BILL MELAMED

MELAMED MANAGEMENT

5757 WILSHIRE BOULEVARD
PENTHOUSE ONE
LOS ANGELES CALIFORNIA 90036-3629
VOX>213.634.8650 FAX>213.634.8651

the creative firm of
Hornall Anderson Design Works
Seattle, Washington
with real-life designers
Jack Anderson, Kathy Saito, & Alan Copeland
created this business card for
Wells Fargo "innoVisions"

Similar cards for related companies create a unified
corporate image.

the creative firm of
Hornall Anderson Design Works
Seattle, Washington
with real-life designers
Jack Anderson, Kathy Saito, & Alan Copeland
created this business card for
innoVentry

Individuality is maintained with slightly different color usage as
well as different flap treatments.

8

J A C K   T O M

D E S I G N   S T U D I O

135 LAZY BROOK ROAD

MONROE   CT   06468

203 / 452 - 0889

the creative firm of
Jack Tom Design
Monroe, Connecticut
with real-life designer
Jack Tom
created this business card for
Jack Tom Design

A very strong effect is the result of bright red used in accordance with bold artwork and type.

2931 104th street, suite c
des moines, iowa 50322

515•270•4858 **ext. 20**
fax: 515•270•0447

TED S. KRUZAN
president

tkruzan@imagetek-inc.com
mobile: 515•238•3229

the creative firm of
Sayles Graphic Design
Des Moines, Iowa
with real-life designer
John Sayles
created this business card for
ImageTek

Computer-chip iconography works well in this logo for a business involved in knowledge management systems. Notice how even the font repeats the dots and curved lines of the overall design.

the creative firm of
Segura Inc.
Chicago, Illinois
with real-life designer
Carlos Segura
created this business card for
Segura Inc.

Three layers of this business card begin with a vellum envelope. Inside, additional printed vellum sheet acts as a cover for the textured card's artwork. Flip side includes all the vitals.

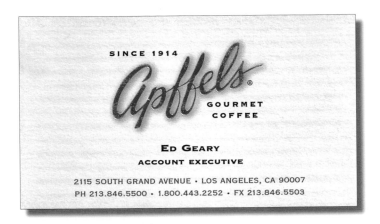

the creative firm of
Barton/Komai/Dunnahoe
Fountain Valley, California
with real-life designers
Joni Parenti & Jeff Barton
created this business card for
Apffels Coffee

Monochromatic, historic photo adorns the back of this gourmet coffee company's card. Front displays the script logo in gold foil stamping.

the creative firm of
Daigle Design
Bainbridge Island, Washington
with real-life designer
Candace Daigle
created this business card for
McKinnon Furniture

Beautifully embossed and "stained" logo is the focal point for McKinnon Furniture, which deals in handcrafted furniture.

the creative firm of
Sayles Graphic Design
Des Moines, Iowa
with real-life designer
John Sayles
created this business card for
1998 Iowa State Fair

Brilliant secondary colors complement splashy artwork.
Appropriately uneven typography adds to the feeling of vitality
and "way too much fun!"

the creative firm of
em dash design
Richmond, Virginia
with real-life designer
Erika Maxwell
created this business card for
Possibilities

Unusually-shaped business card, printed in one color, opens itself to "Possibilities".

des¡gn

harry³ [FOREHAND]

CISNEROS DESIGN inc.
1751-A old pecos trail
santa fe, new mexico, usa 87505
505 983 6677 voice   505 986 2025 fax
cisneros@rt66.com

the creative firm of
Cisneros Design
Santa Fe, New Mexico
with real-life designers
**Fred, Brian, Harry 3, Eric, Heather,
Allane, & Fred Sr.**
created this business card for
Cisneros Design

Black foil stamping in negative space forms this design firm's name on one side of the card. On the other, bright green is unforgettable against a horizontal line that accentuates the card's shape.

the creative firm of
Belyea
Seattle, Washington
with real-life designer
Ron Lars Hansen
created this business card for
Belyea

Very different treatments on opposite sides of this card suggest that the company can communicate on more than one level. A bright orange, painterly image speaks to the artistic audience, while a very clean, much more traditionally-corporate look appeals to those with business on their minds. Square, found twice in the logo, is repeated in larger form on both sides.

marketing

communication

design

belyea.

Patricia Belyea
PRINCIPAL

patricia@belyea.com

1007 Tower Building
1809 Seventh Avenue
Seattle, WA 98101

206.682.4895
FAX 206.623.8912
WEB belyea.com

the creative firm of
**Hornall Anderson
Design Works, Inc.**
Seattle, Washington
with real-life designers
**Jack Anderson, Debra Hampton,
David Bates, & Lisa Cerveny**
created this business card for
Stewart Capital Management

Businesses that deal with money usually want a traditional (firmly established) image. This kind of design rarely lends itself to new ideas. A staid look was avoided here with delicate background textures and almost-bright shadows. Dollar-bill green is offset with a much springier verdant.

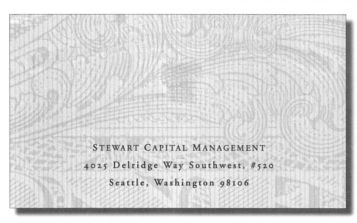

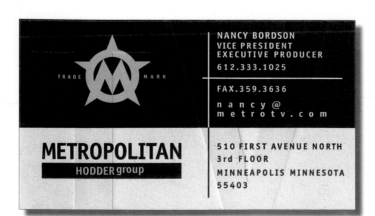

the creative firm of
Compass Design
Minneapolis, Minnesota
with real-life designers
**Mitchell Lindgren, Rich McGowen,
& Tom Arthur**
created this business card for
Metropolitan Hodder Group

Blind debossed "TV", which creates a visual and physical texture, informs the viewer of the cardholder's business. Nice separation of space is employed by hard edges and straight lines.

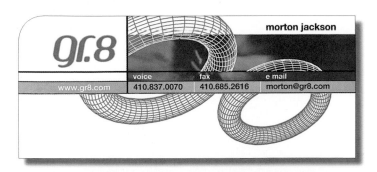

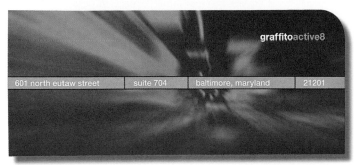

the creative firm of
Gr8
Baltimore, Maryland
with real-life designers
**Morton Jackson, Tim Thompson,
& Chuck Seelye**
created this business card for
Gr8

A successful mix of photographic and drawn images is the main artwork used on this card. Curve of dimensional schematics is cut from a top corner of card.

the creative firm of
Randi Wolf Design, Inc.
Glassboro, New Jersey
with real-life designer
Randi Wolf
created this business card for
Holly Firuta, an aquatic therapist

Flowing curve at bottom edge of card and color choice both wave at the water nature of this business.

the creative firm of
JOE Advertising
Wilton, Connecticut
with real-life designer
Sharon Occhipinti
created these business cards for
J, G, H, C.

Black-and-white photos of each partner, along with each respective name in bold, appear on one side of these interesting business cards. The concentration on punctuation creates a unity across the set of cards while indicating the pictures should be read as words, similar to a rebus.

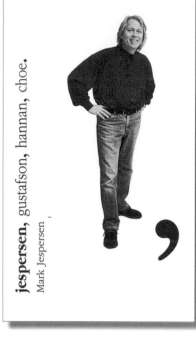

jespersen, gustafson, hannan, choe.
Mark Jespersen

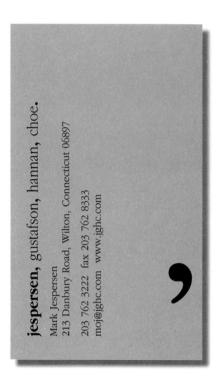

jespersen, gustafson, hannan, choe.
Mark Jespersen
213 Danbury Road, Wilton, Connecticut 06897

203 762 3222   fax 203 762 8333
moj@jghc.com   www.jghc.com

jespersen, gustafson, **hannan**, choe.
Hannah Saunders Hannan

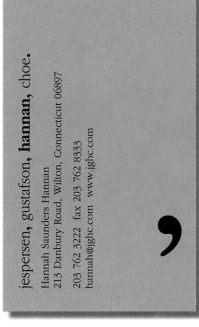

jespersen, gustafson, **hannan**, choe.
Hannah Saunders Hannan
213 Danbury Road, Wilton, Connecticut 06897

203 762 3222 fax 203 762 8333
hannah@jghc.com www.jghc.com

jespersen, gustafson, hannan, **choe.**
Jae Choe, Director of Technology and Media

jespersen, gustafson, hannan, **choe.**
Jae Choe, Director of Technology and Media
213 Danbury Road, Wilton, Connecticut 06897

203 762 3222 fax 203 762 8333
jae@jghc.com www.jghc.com

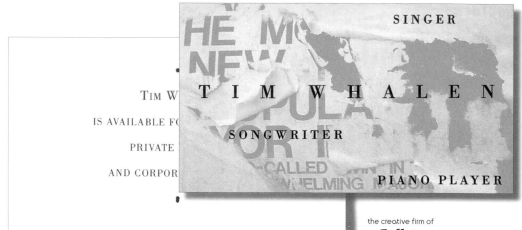

SINGER

TIM WHALEN

SONGWRITER

PIANO PLAYER

TIM W...

IS AVAILABLE FO...

PRIVATE

AND CORPOR...

MANAGER • PROMOTER:

TIM SCOTT

200 SOUTH MIDLAND AVENUE

JOLIET, ILLINOIS 60436

FOR BOOKINGS CALL: 815.741.2804

the creative firm of
Bullet Communications, Inc.
Joliet, Illinois
with real-life designer
Tim Scott
created this business card for
Tim Whalen

The design for this singer, songwriter, and piano player's card has left nothing to chance. The front imagery is a monochromatic collage which would certainly speak to the creative side of his medium. Inside is contact and booking information, and a brief professional bio is found on the card back.

email: info@hillismackey.com • fax: 612.542.8158
1550 Utica Avenue S., Suite 745 • Minneapolis, MN 55416 • www.ia.hillismackey.com

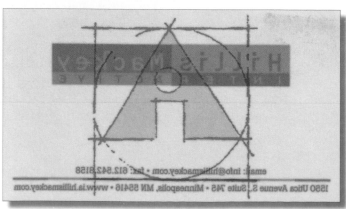

the creative firm of
Hillis Mackey
Minneapolis, Minnesota
with real-life designer
John Hillis
created this business card for
Hillis Mackey Interactive

Printed on both sides, geometric art offering a hand-rendered effect shows through to card front, subtly balancing cleaner and harder-edged textual images.

4557 46TH AVENUE N.E.
SEATTLE, WASHINGTON 98105

VOICE: 206.527.8286
FAX: 206.524.6641

CARY PILLO LASSEN
ILLUSTRATOR

the creative firm of
Belyea
Seattle, Washington
with real-life art director
Patricia Belyea
and designer
Tim Ruszel
created these business cards for
Cary Pillo Lassen

Showcasing the illustrator's talent, examples
of her work appear on four different cards.

4557 46TH AVENUE N.E.
SEATTLE, WASHINGTON 98105

VOICE: 206.527.8286
FAX: 206.524.6641

CARY PILLO LASSEN
ILLUSTRATOR

4557 46TH AVENUE N.E.
SEATTLE, WASHINGTON 98105

VOICE: 206.527.8286
FAX: 206.524.6641

CARY PILLO LASSEN
ILLUSTRATOR

4557 46TH AVENUE N.E.
SEATTLE, WASHINGTON 98105

VOICE: 206.527.8286
FAX: 206.524.6641

CARY PILLO LASSEN
ILLUSTRATOR

cbk:milieu

k u r t   m u e l l e r | r e t a i l   m a n a g e r

seven.four.four.one forsyth boulevard
saint louis, missouri, **usa** six.three.one.zero.five
: three.one.four.eight.six.two.
two.nine.nine.six : [fax] three.one.four.
eight.six.two.two.nine.nine.nine

the creative firm of
**Phoenix
Creative,
St. Louis**
St. Louis, Missouri
with real-life designer
Deborah Finkelstein
created these business cards for
cbk:milieu

An unusual but very modern design was chosen by this high-end furniture retailer. There are two sizes of business cards, one quite large, the other a small square. Both include the same information on glossy card stock printed in two colors with no numerals; the numbers are represented as their word counterparts.

cbk:milieu

seven.four.four.one forsyth boulevard saint louis, missouri, **usa** six.three.one.zero.five
: three.one.four.eight.six.two.two.nine.nine.six
: [fax] three.one.four.eight.six.two.two.nine.nine.nine

christine b. katsantonis | managing director

the creative firm of
em dash design
Richmond, Virginia
with real-life designer
Erika Maxwell
created this business card for
oh wow photography

The "eye of the photographer" reads as letters in the logo, then is repeated and enlarged as background art.

KMTT FM
1100 Olive Way, Suite 1650
Seattle, WA 98101-1827

Phone
206.233.1037

After Hours
206.233.8989

Fax
206.233.8979

E-mail
sales@kmtt.com

Website
http://www.kmtt.com

Chris Kane
Account Executive

An Entercom Station

the creative firm of
Art O Mat Design
Seattle, Washington
with real-life designer
Mark Kaufman
created this business card for
103.7 FM, The Mountain

Radio station's logo incorporates a woodcut texture. Similarly-styled auditory waves are utilized as a background.

2101 locust street st. louis, missouri 63103

dreyfus + associates P H O T O G R A P H Y

t   314 436 1988

f   314 436 7943

dreyfus@stlnet.com

the creative firm of
CUBE Advertising & Design
St. Louis, Missouri
with real-life designer
David Chiow
created this business card for
dreyfus + associates photography

Initial cap comes into focus through the photographer's lens.
Back of card is printed with a faint version of the initial along
with the cardholder's name.

dan dreyfus

the creative firm of
Buttitta Design
Healdsburg, California
with real-life designer
Patti Buttitta
created this business card for
Hanford Company

Business card for a landscaping company includes a beautifully sketched leaf printed in earth tones, incorporating negative space for visual interest.

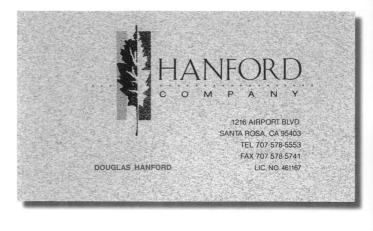

the creative firm of
Sayles Graphic Design
Des Moines, Iowa
with real-life designer
John Sayles
created this business card for
Hotel Fort Des Moines

Illustrative, perspective rendering of Hotel Fort Des Moines is the focal point of this card strong in period typography, indicative of the time the building was constructed.

divine design

| studio inc

president | lynette cortez

twenty seven west twenty fourth street suite *10d, nyc 10010*
telephone *212 924 5009* | facsimile *212 924 0428*

the creative firm of
Divine Design
New York, New York
with real-life designer
Tonya Hudson
created this business card for
Divine Design

Short card with lots of white space draws the
viewer's eye to important typographical information.

the creative firm of
Vestigio
Sra Da Hora, Portugal
with real-life designer
Emanuel Barbosa
created this business card for
Sastre

The visual used in accordance with the name logo
is a monochromatic, partial photo of a man in
motion. The highlighted area of the picture includes
the man's pants, appropriate for a men's fashion
company.

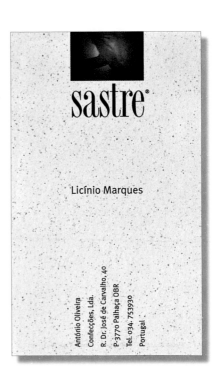

sastre®

Licínio Marques

António Oliveira
Confecções, Lda.
R. Dr. José de Carvalho, 40
P-3770 Palhaça OBR
Tel. 034-753930
Portugal

the creative firm of
Mires Design, Inc.
San Diego, California
created this business card for
ZZYZX

Unique business name is the focal point for this computer equipment company. Infrequently-used letters in a bright yellow make the identity easy to remember.

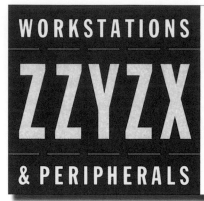

WORKSTATIONS

ZZYZX

& PERIPHERALS

JOHN CAREY

PRESIDENT

5893 OBERLIN DRIVE

SAN DIEGO CA 92121

800 876 7818

619 558 7800

FAX 619 558 8283

E-MAIL:

ZZYZX!SALES@UCSD.EDU

sharpe
models & talent

allison sharpe
831.427.1008 tel
831.427.0525 fax

121 sutphen st
santa cruz, ca
95060

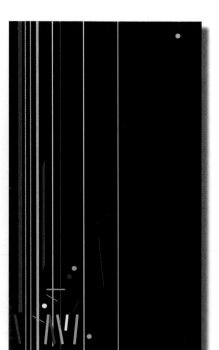

the creative firm of
Kevin Akers—Designer
San Rafael, California
with real-life designer
Kevin Akers
created this business card for
Allison Sharpe

Highly-stylized "models & talent" are represented in primary colors on business card for a talent agent. Reverse side of card is full of kinetic visuals silhouetted against a black background.

the creative firm of
Belyea
Seattle, Washington
with real-life art director
Patricia Belyea
and designer
Christian Salas
created this business card for
Scott Stoll

Eye of the photographer is in the palm of his hand. Yellow, radial gradient with softly blurred edges creates a nice illusion of light.

the creative firm of
Hornall Anderson Design Works
Seattle, Washington
created this business card for
Space Needle

Business card for the Space Needle employs a gold, flecked stock. Good choice of ink colors, making text easy to read, include black and red. Abstract symbol is blind embossed on bottom left corner.

Space Needle
Live The View

Doug Bamford
Marketing

203 6th Avenue North
Seattle, WA 98109-5005
Main: (206) 443-9700
Direct: (206) 443-2161, ext.1432
Fax: (206) 441-7415
E-mail: doug@bamford.com

susan hill
office manager

**the difference
will make you smile**

561 cox road
gastonia, nc 28054

704.865.8521

fax 704.866.0780

301 park street
belmont, nc 28012

704.825.0002

Hannon·orthodontics

the creative firm of
Lyerly Agency
Charlotte, North Carolina
with real-life designer
Leslie Kraemer
created these business cards for
Hannon Orthodontics

A friendly smile, full of straight teeth, helps create an upbeat card for an orthodontist. All letters are lowercase with the exception of the initial cap in the business name. Flip side of business card is printed with humorous definitions of the company name. The distinctiveness of this card might not make the patient's visit more pleasant, but it certainly shows that the doctor is aware of the general public's opinion of a trip to the dentist, and is making an effort to dispel any negativity.

Hannon·orthodontics
\han-ən-ȯr-thə-dänt-iks\
n: 1 a place where everybody loves to smile. 2 where the Doc makes 'em straight.

has an appointment on

❑ mon ❑ tues ❑ wed ❑ thurs ❑ fri

Hannon·orthodontics

561 cox road   gastonia, nc 28054   704.865.8521
301 park street   belmont, nc 28012   704.825.0002

Southern Italian Cuisine

Private Parties · Events

90 Blanchard Street

Seattle, WA 98121

206 · 448 · 6779

fax 206 · 441 · 9513

Lance Wade

the creative firm of
Art O Mat Design
Seattle, Washington
created this business card for
Belltown Billiards

It's obvious by the business card that Belltown Billiards is not just a another "pool hall". Dark purple and silver metallic ink along with an embossed logo speak well for the image of this upscale establishment of billiards, bar, and restaurant.

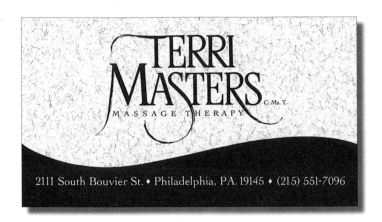

the creative firm of
Randi Wolf Design, Inc.
Glassboro, New Jersey
with real-life designer
Randi Wolf
created this business card for
Terri Masters

Calligraphic letters achieve a hands-on effect for a massage therapist's business card. Gentle curves at the bottom of card succeed in implementing a relaxing rhythm.

the creative firm of
Cathey Associates, Inc.
Dallas, Texas
with real-life designer
Gordon Cathey
created this business card for
Unifications

Unifications is a custom rug design business. A successful weaving of the letters in the company name is depicted by lots of overlapping positive space. An additional balance is executed by repeating the diamond-shaped "i" dots at the bottom of the logo.

Sharon Curtis

Custom Rug Design

2935 Irving Blvd., #204   Dallas, TX 75247   (214) 638-6001   Fax (214) 638-1515

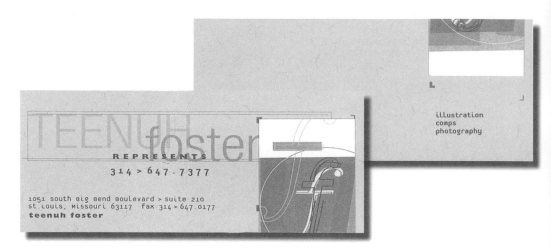

the creative firm of

Phoenix Creative, St. Louis

St. Louis, Missouri

with real-life designer

Deborah Finkelstein

created these business cards for

Teenuh Foster Represents

Individual styles of work are displayed by attaching different stickers to identical business cards. The stickers wrap around the cards to the opposite side where the viewer finds exactly what, as an artist representative, Teenuh Foster Represents: illustration, comps, photography.

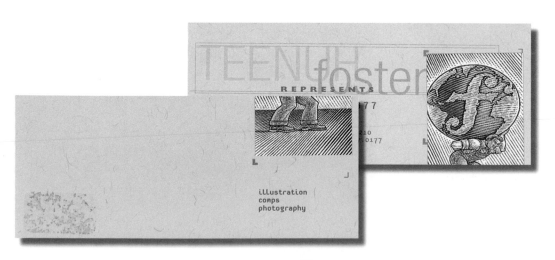

the creative firm of
A-Hill Design
Albuquerque, New Mexico
with real-life designers
Sandy Hill & Emma Roberts
created this business card for
A-Hill Design

Printed label affixed to a luggage check ticket relates directly to
the bellboy icon used in the logo. Name and address are printed as
ownership information, completing the Gestalt.

the creative firm of
**Thibault Paolini
Design Associates**
Portland, Maine
with real-life designer
Judy Paolini
created this business card for
Bix Pix Entertainment

Directional abstracts, including a harlequin border stripe, put
the viewer in mind of the circus, a strong clue that Bix Pix
deals with entertainment. Typewriter font hints at the
occupation of the cardholder, which includes writing.

the creative firm of
Bartels & Company, Inc.
St. Louis, Missouri
created this business card for
NIE Insurance

NIE Insurance's location and business are both represented in their logo. The St. Louis arch is completed in form by a coat hanger; the company specializes in insuring dry cleaners. Flip side of card includes a photo of account rep and phone numbers.

the creative firm of
Gee + Chung Design
San Francisco, California
with real-life art director
Earl Gee
and designers
Earl Gee & Fani Chung
created this business card for
Virtual Vineyards

Logo of lines and shadows includes wine icons and a computer mouse. Memorable shape of card is expressed by inverted, rounded corners on an unusually-narrow palette.

Robert Olson
CHIEF PROPELLER HEAD
rolson@virtualvin.com

Virtual Vineyards

3803 E. Bayshore Road, Suite 175
Palo Alto, CA 94303
Tel: 415.919.1975 ext. 308
Fax: 415.919.1977
www.virtualvin.com

the creative firm of
Adkins/Balchunas
Providence, Rhode Island
with real-life designer
Jerry Balchunas
created this business card for
GiGi's

Free-spirited feeling of this French/American restaurant is translated with the use of calligraphic fonts, gradients, and asymmetrical shapes.

the creative firm of
Belyea
Seattle, Washington
with real-life art director
Patricia Belyea
and designer
Christian Salas
created this business card for
Maison de France

One color printing contributes to the elegant image of a retail store specializing in "the art of French living". Ornate fleur de lis is reversed out of a solid background and crosses over into positive space. Card back makes locating the store easy with a map in which the store is represented by its logo.

the creative firm of
Muccino Design Group
San Jose, California
with real-life designers
Alfredo Muccino & Stacy Guidice
created this business card for
Plan B Communications

Very narrow card divides information into a fine balance of boxes Mondrian-style. Two-color printing appears as three with the card color effectually considered in the design.

the creative firm of
Fuze
San Francisco, California
with real-life designers
Tom Sieu & Tim Carpenter
created this business card for
Christina Robbins Represents

Loosely applied painterly elements are offset by hard lines giving the appearance of masking tape edges. Typography mimics the background imagery.

No man but a
blockhead ever
wrote except
for money

-SAMUEL JOHNSON

MIKE PURSWELL / WRITER / PRODUCER

When you steal
from one author,
it's plagiarism;
if you steal
from many,
it's research

-MAXIM MAXIMOVICH LITVINOV

MIKE PURSWELL / WRITER / PRODUCER

the creative firm of
VNU Design
Nashville, Tennessee
with real-life designer
Jim Viennean
created these business cards for
Mike Purswell

Folded copywriter's business card is characterized by quotes from famous authors printed in a rough typewriter font. Card holder's initials are highlighted within each quote by use of a second color of ink. Inside, the viewer finds the technical info.

ADVERTISING COPY
CORPORATE WRITING
WEBSITE DEVELOPMENT

208 REIDHURST AVENUE, NASHVILLE, TENNESSEE 37203
T 615-320-1962 F 615-321-5952

MIKE PURSWELL / WRITER / PRODUCER

In matters of
true importance,
style is
everything

-OSCAR WILDE

MIKE PURSWELL / WRITER / PRODUCER

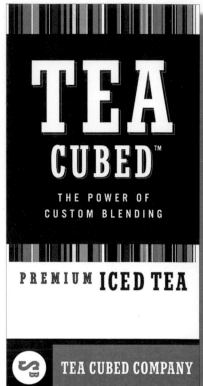

the creative firm of
Sparc
Chicago, Illinois
with real-life designer
Richard Cassis
created this business card for
Tea Cubed Company

Computer illustration visually expresses the name of this company on the front of its folded business card. Strong colors and lots of reversed type are sure to leave a memorable impression to whomever the card is given.

TEA CUBED COMPANY

Premium leaves blended to perfection.

Smooth, refreshing teas at a reasonable price.

Service beyond compare.

the creative firm of
Phoenix Creative, St. Louis
St. Louis, Missouri
with real-life designer
Deborah Finkelstein
created this business card for
Ham on Rye Technologies

Creating an identity for a highly-technological company can be tricky. It needs to appeal to those who need the service (here interactive technologies) but might be a little intimidated by the media. On the other hand, a focus on the future and cutting edge information is important. "Ham on Rye" is an image with which almost everyone can relate while it suggests a service-oriented company. Atomic images describe the forward-thinking aspect of the business.

the creative firm of
Sayles Graphic Design
Des Moines, Iowa
with real-life designer
John Sayles
created this business card for
1999 Iowa State Fair

Colorful graphics indicative of movement reiterate the theme of the
1999 Iowa State Fair, "Knock Yourself Out".

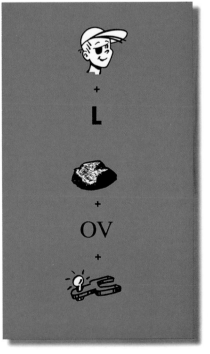

the creative firm of
Kevin Akers—Designer
San Rafael, California
with real-life designer
Kevin Akers
created this personal card for
Joelle Rokovich

Calling card (the kind you leave—not the kind you use with a phone) is printed with the owner's
name on one side; the flip side has her name represented in rebus fashion.

SPECTRUM
BRANDS

Lee Brown
Region Manager

22893 Antique Lane
P.O. Box 1198
New Caney, Texas 77357

281.399.1199 800.468.0525 ext.2539
fax 281.399.1833
e-mail wlb1946@worldnet.att.net
www.spectrumbrands.com

the creative firm of
Phoenix Creative, St. Louis
St. Louis, Missouri
with real-life designer
Tyler Small
created these business cards for
United Industries/Spectrum Brands

Chemical company logo includes two of its three corporate colors, orange and green, combining to form the remaining one, purple. This is interesting from a design standpoint because partial elements within the colors of orange and green, red and blue respectively, are what form purple. Backs of cards are printed full bleed with one of the aforementioned colors.

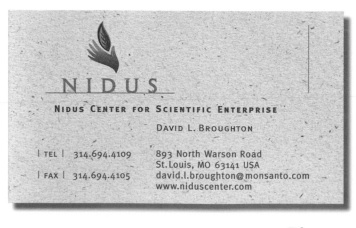

N I D U S

NIDUS CENTER FOR SCIENTIFIC ENTERPRISE

DAVID L. BROUGHTON

| TEL | 314.694.4109   893 North Warson Road
| FAX | 314.694.4105   St. Louis, MO 63141 USA
david.l.broughton@monsanto.com
www.niduscenter.com

the creative firm of
Phoenix Creative, St. Louis
St. Louis, Missouri
with real-life designer
Ed Mantels-Seeker
created this business card for
Surfacine Development Company

A focus on things natural permeate this card for a company whose business is antimicrobial technology. A leaf and hand in colors of gold and green help create a feeling of harmony between science and nature.

DESIGNER ❦ ILLUSTRATOR

JULIE RUMSEY

4512 EAST DRIFTWOOD
MERIDIAN, IDAHO 83642
208.377.4013

the creative firm of
Crain Design Office
Simi Valley, California
created this business card for
Julie Crain

Freelance artist, who specializes in painting murals and tiles, offers examples of her work right on her business card. Illustrations of various fruits and vegetables coordinate nicely with a font using exaggerated thicks and thins.

the creative firm of
Kevin Akers—Designer
San Rafael, California
with real-life designer
Kevin Akers
created this business card for
Go Manufacture

The strength of this design is found in its use of color. Obviously the company's name, GO, was to be the focus; traffic light red, yellow, and green (stop, caution, and GO) were chosen. They appear even bolder against a black background, and the green GO is reinforced by placement of the green light inside the letter O.

Joseph Vitug
Engineering Manager

GO MANUFACTURE

3280 Lac Bleu Court
San Jose, CA USA 95148

P 408.532.9681
F 408.532.9781
email: jvitug@gomanufacture.com

GO

the creative firm of
Pinpoint Communications
Deerfield Beach, Florida
with real-life designers
J. Dudley Davenport & Jonathan Gouthier
created this business card for
Falcon Hedge Fund

Colorful, illustrative logo is embossed on card front. Card back
is printed with the logo in one color, full bleed, and enlarged.

GLEN T. VITTOR
INVESTMENT MANAGER

FALCON
HEDGE FUNDS

5200 TOWN CENTER CIRCLE, SUITE 303
BOCA RATON, FLORIDA 33486
PH 561 447-4888   FX 561 447-4382

the creative firm of
The Flowers Group
San Diego, California
with real-life designer
Cory Sheehan
created this business card for
Co·Opportunities

Directional left border is comprised of business name and triangle which serves as an arrow.
It draws the eye directly to the repeated business name, this time within the logo. Back of
card is printed with the characters of the logo full bleed.

CORY SHEEHAN
ART DIRECTOR

CO-OPPORTUNITIES
The Partnership Marketing Company

6244 FERRIS SQUARE
SAN DIEGO, CA 92121
TEL 619 / 558 / 6890
FAX 619 / 558 / 6903
adman@adnc.com

STUDIO **E**

CREATORS OF EXCEPTIONAL PLACES™

JEFFREY L. BLYDENBURGH, AIA
Major Accounts Director

211 North Broadway, Sixth Floor
St. Louis, Missouri 63102
Tel: 314 421 2000   Fax: 314 621 0944
E-Mail: jeffrey.blydenburgh@hok.com

LOS ANGELES • ORLANDO

the creative firm of
Phoenix Creative, St. Louis
St. Louis, Missouri
with real-life designer
Deborah Finkelstein
created this business card for
HOK Architects/Studio E

Three versions of the letter "e" are incorporated within a cube,
representing both the company's name, Studio E, and business,
architecture.

Lamar Taylor
President
Utah WebWorks, Inc.

voice: 801-578-9020
fax: 801-578-9019

180 South 300 West, Suite 220   lamar@utahwebworks.com
Salt Lake City, Utah 84101   www.utahwebworks.com

the creative firm of
HM Design
Salt Lake City, Utah
with real-life designers
Dave Malone & Lisa Critchfield
created this business card for
Utah Webworks, Inc.

Artwork symbolizing gear parts is rendered with offset circles
and uneven typography, indicating a frenzy of activity.

personify

www.*personify*.com

50 Osgood Place, Suite 100
San Francisco, California 94133

T 415 / 782 2050
F 415 / 544 0318

the creative firm of
Hornall Anderson Design Works
Seattle, Washington
with real-life designers
**Jack Anderson, Debra McCloskey,
& Holly Finlayson**
created these business cards for
Personify

Individual icons in the top left corner of each card represent
individual executives in this software manufacturing company.
The card back is printed full bleed blue and has the person's
name in orange yellow.

personify

www.*personify*.com

50 Osgood Place, Suite 100
San Francisco, California 94133

T 415 / 782 2050
F 415 / 544 0318

personify

[EILEEN HICKEN GITTINS   ]
ceo

415 / 782 2055
egittins@personify.com

personify

www.*personify*.com

50 Osgood Place, Suite 100
San Francisco, California 94133

T 415 / 782 2050
F 415 / 544 0318

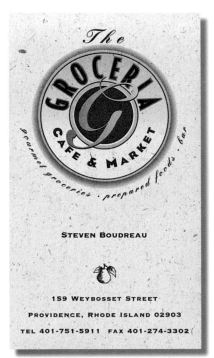

STEVEN BOUDREAU

159 WEYBOSSET STREET
PROVIDENCE, RHODE ISLAND 02903
TEL 401-751-5911 FAX 401-274-3302

Dine, drink, and shop

...gourmet style.

the creative firm of
Adkins/Balchunas
Providence, Rhode Island
with real-life designers
Jerry Balchunas & Michelle Phaneuf
created this business card for
The Groceria

Circular logo has text in the form of initial cap in script and remaining text in sans serif font. Reverse side of card is full bleed with serif text reversed out of dark blue.

the creative firm of
Janet Payne Graphic Designer
Hopewell, New Jersey
with real-life designer
Janet Payne
created this business card for
Trigram Touch Therapies, Inc.

Using the most important touch in all history of mankind, interpreted by Michelangelo in The Creation of Adam, the artwork on this card hints at the life giving power behind touch therapy.

TRIGRAM
TOUCH THERAPIES, INC.

Diane Schrak
Certified Massage Therapist
and Associates

Mallard Creek Village
130 Almshouse Road, Suite 301
Richboro, Pennsylvania 18954
215-357-1444

the creative firm of
Belyea
Seattle, Washington
with real-life art director
Patricia Belyea
and designer
Ron Lars Hansen
created this business card for
VHPR

Printed in purple and avocado, full bleed flip side shows a compass, that includes the logo, showing the client the way to go.

GUIDING COMMUNICATION

the creative firm of
Shelby Designs & Illustrates
Oakland, California
with real-life designers
Shelby Putnam Tupper, & Susan Rothman
created this business card for
Michael Pozzan Winery

Great background texture is a photographic rendering of a grape leaf. Text is printed in violet over the gold background. Cluster of grapes is derived from a scratchboard illustration.

Michael Pozzan
W I N E R Y

MICHAEL POZZAN

ST. HELENA HWY
NAPA VALLEY

POST OFFICE BOX 2121
ORINDA · CA · 94563

T: 510·235·8712
F: 925·283·0552

the creative firm of
Gee + Chung Design
San Francisco, California
with real-life art director and designer
Earl Gee
and illustrator
Robert Pastrana
created this business card for
Xinet

Uniquely-angled edges are the beginning for this out-of-the-ordinary, folded business card. Four color printing on coated stock is accented by metallic gold ink. Artwork and typography treatments are reminiscent of the Cubist movement.

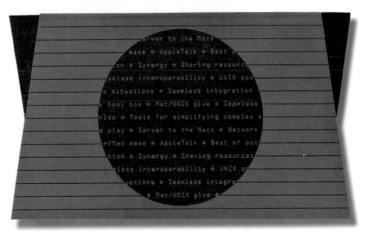

the creative firm of
Phoenix Creative, St. Louis
St. Louis, Missouri
with real-life designer
Deborah Finkelstein
created this business card for
Ferguson & Katzman Photography

This business card is a good study in typography. Slightly debossed initial caps dominate the remaining sans serif font which is printed in muted tones and presented in different styles and orientations.

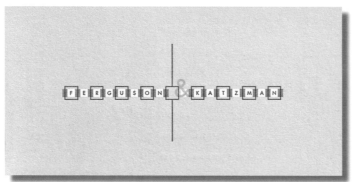

Rick Zaidan
Photographer

1668 State Road
Cuyahoga Falls, Ohio 44223
330-920-8142
Fax 330-920-8125
zphotogr@neo.lrun.com

the creative firm of
Louis & Partners
Bath, Ohio
created this business card for
Zaidan Photography

Card front displays all pertinent information in a well-balanced format. Card back is a charming photo of a bow-tied boy and his camera, leaving the impression Rick Zaidan has been a photographer (and maybe a snappy dresser) all his life.

ITALIA

206 623 1917

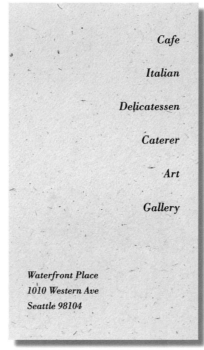

Cafe

Italian

Delicatessen

Caterer

Art

Gallery

Waterfront Place
1010 Western Ave
Seattle 98104

the creative firm of
**Hornall Anderson
Design Works**
Seattle, Washington
with real-life designers
Jack Anderson, Julia LaPine
created this business card for
Italia Restaurant & Wine Bar

Illustrative logo of a cluster of grapes complements clean-edged font chosen for the business name. A nice choice was made to repeat the curve of one of the grapes in the phone number's baseline. Turning the card over, one find's company descriptors and address.

the creative firm of
**Phoenix Creative,
St. Louis**
St. Louis, Missouri
with real-life designer
Deborah Finkelstein
created this business card for
Alpine Shop

Casual, but fun, card for an outdoor retailer uses outdoorsy icons and natural colors. Typographical execution is in excellent relation with images; it contains a mixture of capitals and lowercase letters, none of them exactly aligned.

ALPINE
SHOP

601 EAST LOCKWOOD { ST. LOUIS, MISSOURI } 63119

314.962.7715
(phOnE)

LisA HOLLenBECK

Lhollenbeck@primary.net

{ fAx] 314.962.7718
www.alpineshOp.com [weB]

the creative firm of
D4
Philadelphia, Pennsylvania
created these business cards for
D4

Similar cards use separate texture fills for the numeral in the company name—generally in direct relation to the card holder's occupation. Reverse side shows the business name reversed out of full bleed purple.

TV | RADIO | PRINT | WEB

Suzanne Hatfield
President

4100 Main Street, Suite 210
Philadelphia, PA 19127-1623
215.483.4555 fax 215.483.4554
http://www.d4tv.com

TV | RADIO | PRINT | WEB

Wicky W. Lee
Print Art Director

4100 Main Street, Suite 210
Philadelphia, PA 19127-1623
215.483.4555 fax 215.483.4554
http://www.d4tv.com

TV | RADIO | PRINT | WEB

Terri Blatch
Producer/Media Architect

4100 Main Street, Suite 210
Philadelphia, PA 19127-1623
215.483.4555 fax 215.483.4554
http://www.d4tv.com

TV | RADIO | PRINT | WEB

Beverly Littlewood
Video Art Director

4100 Main Stree
Philadelphia, PA
215.483.4555 fa
http://www.d4

46

Susan L. Bragg, Ph.D.
Principal

SpectrAlliance, Inc.

7534 Watson Road
St. Louis, MO 63119
314.962.4555 Phone
314.962.4385 Fax
sbragg@s-alliance.com E-Mail

the creative firm of
CUBE Advertising & Design
St. Louis, Missouri
with real-life designers
David Chiow & Kevin Hough
created this business card for
SpectrAlliance, Inc.

Directional logo is comprised of company's initial
caps in abstraction. Used as an important element on
the business card, it guides the viewer's eye directly
to the name of this spectrometer manufacturer.

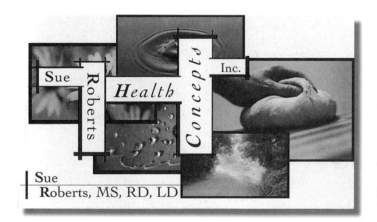

the creative firm of
Sayles Graphic Design
Des Moines, Iowa
with real-life designer
John Sayles
created this business card for
Sue Roberts Health Concepts

Health consultant's business is visually translated on her card
with photographs strong in a natural theme.

1515 Linden Street Des Moines, Iowa 50309
Suite 220
Fax: (515) 247-0016 Phone (515) 247-0014

sue@healthconceptsinc.com
www.healthconceptsinc.com

the creative firm of
Jack Tom Design
Monroe, Connecticut
with real-life designer
Jack Tom
created this business card for
Rick Mariani Photography

Copper foil stamping accomplishes the successful play
between positive and negative space in this photographer's
logo comprised of his initials.

RICK MARIANI
PHOTOGRAPHY

224 Mississippi Street
San Francisco, CA 94107

Studio: 415/864-7427
Fax: 415/864-0542

E-Mail:
RicksPix@aol.com

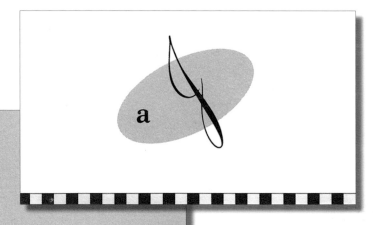

the creative firm of
Kevin Akers—Designer
San Rafael, California
with real-life designer
Kevin Akers
created this business card for
Amelia Johnson

Classy, folded business card offers unexpected mix of fonts in
logo on cover. The striped/boxed bottom border maintains
continuity between front and inside.

AMELIA JOHNSON   503/648-3807

MARKETING COMMUNICATIONS
PUBLIC RELATIONS

2832 SOUTHEAST CAMWALL DRIVE
HILLSBORO, OREGON 97123

the creative firm of
Janet Payne Graphic Designer
Hopewell, New Jersey
with real-life designer
Janet Payne
created this business card for
Randy Payne

Architectural rendering of a beautifully-designed wooden home fits well in the horizontal orientation of the business card. Occupation, carpenter, is force justified across card width with extra kerning.

the creative firm of
CRSR Designs Inc.
Kingston, New York
with real-life designer
Constance Snyder
created this business card for
CRSR Designs Inc.

If an image created with Gestalt in mind is an entity with a sum greater than the value of its individual parts, this background surely represents what happens when the individual parts are deconstructed.

the creative firm of
Boelts Bros. Associates
Tucson, Arizona
created this business card for
Southwest School of Music

The fact that this school is in the southwestern United States is very important to the graphics on the card. Colors and iconography both hint at the location and culture.

the creative firm of
AERIAL
San Francisco, California
with real-life designers
Tracy Moon & Stephanie West
created this business card for
Collage Salon

An oval is an uncommon shape for a business card for several reasons, cost and rolodex storage among the rest, but it is very distinctive and therefore memorable. This oval is especially unique in that it must be turned approximately 10° to produce a 90° text line. The turning gives the card an asymmetrical effect—even more memorable.

LIFE**STYLE**SALON

joan townsend

1570 La Pradera Drive Campbell, Ca 95008-1533

telephone 408.378.1355 facsimile 408.378.2774

www.collagesalon.com

relax@collagesalon.com

METAPHASE DESIGN GROUP

1266 Andes Boulevard

Saint Louis, Missouri 63132

Telephone: 314 432 0300

Facsimile: 314 432 7991

BRYCE G. RUTTER, PH.D.

Principal

the creative firm of
Ed Mantels-Seeker
St. Louis, Missouri
with real-life designer
Ed Mantels-Seeker
created this business card for
Metaphase

Geometric perfection in its logo design represents this
industrial design group well. Rather neutral hues are offset by
the discretionary use of red.

the creative firm of
Adkins/Balchunas
Providence, Rhode Island
with real-life designers
Jerry Balchunas & Matthew Fernberger
created this business card for
107 Ocean Bistro

Ocean colors of green and blue were chosen for the card of
this seafood restaurant. Business name is made the focal
point by relative size and departure from remaining clean
typography. The name is further dimensionalized with the aid
of a drop shadow.

Edward L. Shore

President & CEO

500 Callahan Road

North Kingstown

Rhode Island 02852

Phone 401.295.2533 x777

Fax 401.295.5984

Cell 401.965.2336

the creative firm of
Adkins/Balchunas
Providence, Rhode Island
with real-life designers
Susan DeAngelis & Michelle Phaneuf
created this business card for
Icon

Ray of light cuts into the logo of this architectural lighting manufacturer. "Light" is rendered with the use of a gradient fill in the logo letters. Also noteworthy is the heavy stock chosen for this card.

the creative firm of
Adkins/Balchunas
Providence, Rhode Island
with real-life designers
Jerry Balchunas & Matthew Fernberger
created this business card for
Lemongrass

Well-integrated shades of yellow and green are a visual interpretation of this Asian restaurant's name. Calligraphy and italic font are a good mix.

Lemongrass
Asian Inspired Contemporary Cuisine

John T. Buffa

1363 Old Northern Blvd., Roslyn, NY 11756
phone: 516-625-4223 fax: 516-625-4387

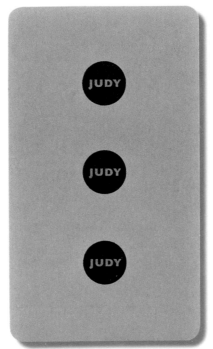

the creative firm of
Lynn Schulte Design
Minneapolis, Minnesota
with real-life designer
Lynn Schulte
created this business card for
Judy MacManus

The viewer can almost hear Cary Grant reading the repeated logo on the card back.

the creative firm of
Belyea
Seattle, Washington
with real-life art director
Patricia Belyea
and designer
Adrianna Jumping Eagle
created this business card for
Kelly McCombs

Simple card is designed well with the manipulation of only four elements. Strong individuality for this artist is produced by business card shape and size.

the creative firm of
Mayer & Myers
Philadelphia, Pennsylvania
with real-life designers
Nancy Mayer & Greg Simmons
created this business card for
Jamie Rothstein

A variety of flowers is an apropos background on this floral designer's card. The monochromatic, lavender photo is flipped on the card's reverse and printed in magenta. Text divisions are defined by hairlines differing in lengths.

the creative firm of
Ed Mantels-Seeker
St. Louis, Missouri
with real-life designer
Ed Mantels-Seeker
created these business cards for
Ziezo

The name of this women's clothing boutique **almost** makes it in its entirety on the card's front. The splashy, painterly fashion in which the name is expressed is portrayed in three different versions, creating a stronger impression than a single card could.

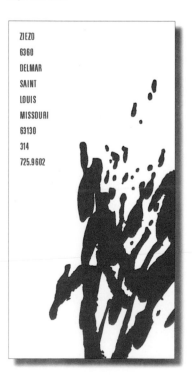

Bloom Smith

Landscape Rejuvenation ▪ Design & Installation

Karen Olson Smith

214.348.0156   mobil 214.202.5983   bloom@airmail.net

the creative firm of
Cathey Associates, Inc.
Dallas, Texas
with real-life designer
Matt Westapher
created this business card for
BloomSmith

Aqua accents highlight purple type. Obviously, a bloomsmith is one
whose business it is to make things bloom-good play on owner's last
name.

the creative firm of
Kevin Akers—Designer
San Rafael, California
with real-life designer
Kevin Akers
created this business card for
Blue Leaf Design

Bright colors are printed on coated stock for this outdoor product
designer's card. Reverse side is printed full bleed with a leaf texture.

the creative firm of
**Hornall Anderson
Design Works**
Seattle, Washington
with real-life designers
**Jack Anderson, Julie Keenan, &
Mary Chin Hutchison**
created this business card for
Rod Ralston Photography Studio

Reverse image on opposite sides of the camera's lens is the focal point on one side of this card; the other employs it, enlarged, as a full bleed background texture.

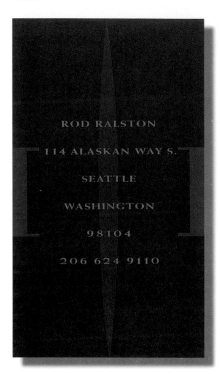

KATIE SIMS
Director, Communications

One Stimson Lane
Woodinville, WA 98072
206-488-4682
Fax 206-488-4657

the creative firm of
Hornall Anderson Design Works
Seattle, Washington
with real-life designers
**John Hornall, Debra McCloskey,
& Mary Chin Hutchison**
created this business card for
Columbia Crest Winery

Domestic and agricultural image is effected with woodcut-style artwork of winery and vineyard.

the creative firm of
Bartels & Company, Inc.
St. Louis, Missouri
created this business card for
Cheapy Smokes

Discount tobacco store uses an updated version of the cigar-store
Indian in its logo.

the creative firm of
Phoenix Creative, St. Louis
St. Louis, Missouri
with real-life designer
Ed Mantels-Seeker
created this business card for
Art Classics, Ltd.

The precision applied in this company's business, framemaking, is
rendered in the geometrically-dynamic logo.

the creative firm of
Randi Wolf Design, Inc.
Glassboro, New Jersey
with real-life designer
Randi Wolf
created this business card for
Tri-State Wallcoverings

Printed wallpaper textures, including a border at card top,
indicate the card holder's business. Initial logo is comprised of
an S in the form of a wallpaper roll inside a foil stamped T.
That sounds difficult to execute, but it works here.

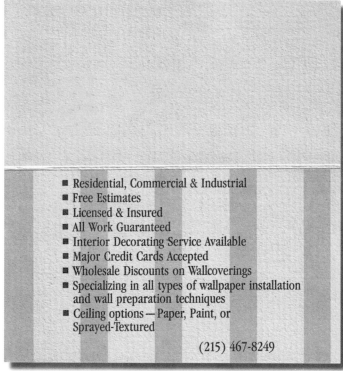

the creative firm of
em dash design
Richmond, Virginia
with real-life designer
Erika K. Maxwell
created this business card for
Gregory D. Small & Associates

Plainly, the gears are always turning within this consultant's
head. Repetition of profile icon successfully completes the
cog image.

the creative firm of
Ellen Bruss Design
Denver, Colorado
with real-life art director
Ellen Bruss
and designer
Charles Carpenter
plus illustrator
G. Carr
created this business card for
Cuisine Chez Vous

Square, folded card with apt illustrations personalize this chef's business card. Information is inside; repeated stripes from the front of card cover the back.

the creative firm of

Adkins/Balchunas

Providence, Rhode Island

with real-life designers

Susan DeAngelis, Jerry Balchunas

created this business card for

Red Bowl

Velveteen-looking, strong red card stock is printed over with metallic silver ink, producing a visually-tactile card.

 David A. Pruett

pruett@goodnet.com

404 South Mill, Ste.C201

Tempe, Arizona 85281

Fax:602.303.0550

Tel:602.303.9500 #225

GoodNet

the creative firm of

After Hours Creative

Phoenix, Arizona

created this business card for

GoodNet

Colors not usually chosen for corporate America include neon green and royal blue. Imagery dealing with various forms of information (multimedia, finances, politics, technology, world travel, things international) leaves the impression of a fast-paced, up-to-date business.

the creative firm of
Ellen Bruss Design
Denver, Colorado
with real-life art director
Ellen Bruss
and designer
Jason C. Otero
created this business card for
Manhattan Grill

Dimensional letters are created with gradient fills, white outlines, and, in the background depicting shadows, duplicate letters in black, slightly offset.

the creative firm of
Hornall Anderson Design Works
Seattle, Washington
with real-life designers
Jack Anderson, Kathy Saito, Julie Lock, Ed Lee, Heidi Favour, & Virginia Le
created this business card for
Ground Zero

Ground Zero, the beginning point, starts with a distinctive business card size. The "prohibitive" O in the company name is enlarged on the red side of the card and printed with the faintest shadow. Circle in letter O works as a design element within the typography i.e. phone numbers.

the creative firm of
Shelby Designs & Illustrates
Oakland, California
with real-life designer
Shelby Putnam Tupper
created this business card for
The Bock Company

Vertical business card imitates logo orientation.
Metallic silver ink works well with dominant hues of
green ink and card stock.

The Bock Company
2998 Washington Street
San Francisco · CA · 94115

TEL 415·751·7569
FAX 415·751·1633

bockco@pacbell.net

Jeff Bock

8935 Manchester
Saint Louis
Missouri 63144

Telephone: 961-1985
Area Code 314

the creative firm of
Phoenix Creative, St. Louis
St. Louis, Missouri
with real-life designer
Ed Mantels-Seeker
created this business card for
The Gifted Gardener

Leaf icons used as bullets to separate text areas are a
subtle touch to the business card of this company that offers
gardening accessories and gifts. A bee, the gardener's best
friend, bleeds off bottom of card indicating flight and
movement.

beautiful antique wall finishes

faithfully recreated

tree laurita studio

2715 larimer street denver colorado 80205

2 9 3 3 9 2 1

the creative firm of
Ellen Bruss Design
Denver, Colorado
created this business card for
Tree Laurita Studio

Deeply-blind embossed logo highlights this card. An excellent choice
was made with lined-textured stock as the business produces
"beautiful antique walls finishes", and does wall painting and murals.

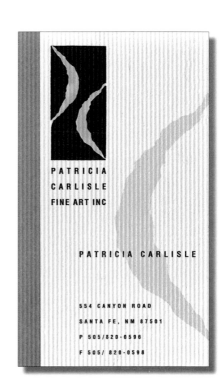

PATRICIA
CARLISLE
FINE ART INC

PATRICIA CARLISLE

554 CANYON ROAD

SANTA FE, NM 87501

P 505/820-0596

F 505/ 820-0598

the creative firm of
A-Hill Design
Albuquerque, New Mexico
with real-life designer
Sandy Hill
created this business card for
Patricia Carlisle Fine Art Inc.

Painterly logo imitates a watercolor wash as it **almost**
mirrors shapes that form the initials of the business
owner.

MARKETING
COMMUNICATIONS

cf2GS

BILL FRITSCH

1008
WESTERN AVE
SUITE 201
SEATTLE, WA
98104

206 223-6464
FAX 223-2765

the creative firm of
Hornall Anderson Design Works
Seattle, Washington
with real-life designers
Jack Anderson & David Bates
created these business cards for
Cf2GS

Different collages of the company's letters and numeral are printed full bleed on the backs of these cards. The card with a collage highlighting a particular initial belongs to the respective partner whose last name begins with that letter. This treatment offers both cohesiveness in the company's image and individuality for each partner.

Peter Douglas
President and CEO

salusmedia
14529 Dickens Street • Sherman Oaks • California 91403
tel 818.990.0607 • fax 818.990.4408
pdouglas@salus.net

the creative firm of
AERIAL
San Francisco, California
created this business card for
Salus Media, Inc.

A nice relationship within the integration of colors is created with the orange orbit symbol connecting both words, while the blue invades the orange text by dotting the i.

the creative firm of
AERIAL
San Francisco, California
with real-life designers
Tracy Moon, Stephanie West, & Kimberly Cross
created this business card for
Tribe Pictures

Thicker-than-usual stock has an uncommon flexibility. Rounded corners and slightly debossed printing add texture to an already tactile card.

scott Robbe

TRiBE

Tribe pictures

244 Main
chatham, NJ 07928
tel 973/635/2660
Fax 973/635/2654
home Office 212/545/0697
scott@tribepictures.com
www.tribepictures.com

TRiBE

[m o v i n g]
Pictures

the creative firm of
Black Bean Studios
Boston, Massachusetts
with real-life designer
Alisha Vera
created this business card for
Gimbels Wine

With no existing logo when this card was designed, Gimbel's identity was developed using their existing signage—contemporary yet whimsical. Stock chosen was a heavy vellum allowing the full-bleed artwork from the card back to be seen through to the card front.

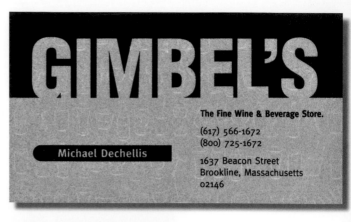

the creative firm of
WaterWork Art
San Francisco, California
with real-life designer
Brenda Phillips
created this business card for
Cafe Trevi

Shadow treatment is unexpected because it is actually lighter than the object it mimics. Created with colors found elsewhere on the card, cream and a percentage of black, it's very effective even though the logo is tonally darker.

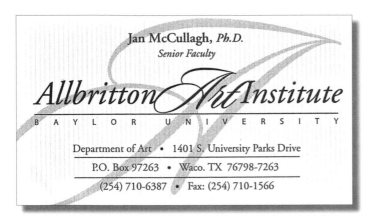

Jan McCullagh, *Ph.D.*
Senior Faculty

Allbritton Art Institute
B A Y L O R   U N I V E R S I T Y

Department of Art • 1401 S. University Parks Drive
P.O. Box 97263 • Waco. TX 76798-7263
(254) 710-6387 • Fax: (254) 710-1566

the creative firm of
Terry M. Roller, Graphic Designer
Hewitt, Texas
with real-life designer
Terry M. Roller
created this business card for
Allbritton Art Institute

Script and italic fonts succeed in unity while highlighting "Art",
this institution's business. Script A is enlarged and printed as a
background shadow.

the creative firm of
HW Design
Marina Del Rey, California
with real-life designer
Hillary Weiss
created this business card for
Rob Shanahan Photography

Very heavy card gives an even more substantial impression
when printed full bleed black. Logo incorporates a camera's
aperture into a subtle eye.

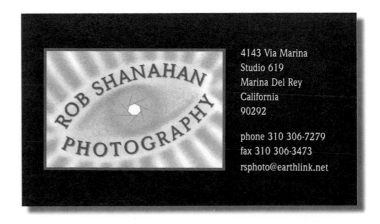

4143 Via Marina
Studio 619
Marina Del Rey
California
90292

phone 310 306-7279
fax 310 306-3473
rsphoto@earthlink.net

the creative firm of
Sheehan Design
Seattle, Washington
created this business card for
Shamrock Associates

There is no question that the holder of this card's business is money. Artwork from U.S. currency is interpreted in "dollar-green" ink. Typography and fibered stock mimic that on folding cash. The name of this real estate and mortgage investment company is visually repeated by using a shamrock for the o in the company name—also created in money-artwork style.

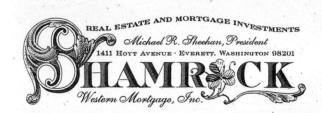

REAL ESTATE AND MORTGAGE INVESTMENTS

Michael R. Sheehan, President

1411 HOYT AVENUE · EVERETT, WASHINGTON 98201

SHAMR CK

Western Mortgage, Inc.

TOLLFREE	(800) 959-3329
LOCAL	(206) 303-8201
FAX	(206) 303-0501

James Cannon Boyce   Writer

B O Y Ⓒ E

16 Ship's Bell Road
Gloucester, MA 01930
P. 508.283.7270
F. 508.282.1865
M. 508.954.8683

the creative firm of
Adkins/Balchunas
Providence, Rhode Island
created this business card for
James Boyce

C in cardholder's name is circled, forming a copyright symbol. The card belongs to a copywriter. (Copyright, copywrite... get it?)

Portland

Seattle

San Francisco

Los Angeles

Doug Campbell

Director, Broadcast Division

1750 NW Front St.

Suite 102

Portland, OR 97209

www.csidigital.com

Tel: 503/224-6626

Fax: 503/228-0132

dougc@csidigital.com

San Francisco

Seattle

Portland

Los Angeles

Mary Fenstermaker

Seattle

Portland

San Francisco

Los Angeles

Elizabeth Jewell

Marketing Director

400 North 34th St.

Suite 201

Seattle, WA 98103

www.csidigital.com

Tel: 206/674-5203

Fax: 206/632-7127

elizabethj@csidigital.com

the creative firm of
**Hornall Anderson
Design Works**
Seattle, Washington
with real-life designers
Jack Anderson & John Anicker
created these business cards for
CSI Digital

Very similar cards are different colors for
different individuals. List of office locations are
found on the left of card front. Cardholder's
location is highlighted.

Los Angeles

Seattle

Portland

San Francisco

Jennifer M. Moore

S.W. Region Sales Coordinator

11845 W. Olympic Blvd.

Suite 640

Los Angeles, CA 90064

www.csidigital.com

310/444-5279

Fax: 310/444-5913

jmoore@csidigital.com

the creative firm of
Yamamoto Moss
Minneapolis, Minnesota
with real-life designer
Gretchen Blase
created this business card for
Yamamoto Moss

The color scheme for the artwork on the business card's back is predominantly complimentary using orange and blue—splashes of green and red are thrown in for good measure. Imagery & iconography modify the descriptor line of endless imagination.

B

D

Annette Jannotta
Designer

Beckson Design Associates
933 North La Brea Ave. Suite 300
Los Angeles, CA 90038
323.874.6144 Fax 323.874.6148
ajannotta@becksondesign.com

A

the creative firm of
James Robie Design Associates
Los Angeles, California
with real-life creative director
James Robie
and design director & designer
Wayne Fujita
created this business card for
Beckson Design Associates

Large areas of solid white allow great focus on sparsely-used bright orange letters.

Denise Drayton Senior Trainer
denise@exponents.org

People Living With AIDS/HIV
Leadership Training Institute
A Program of Exponents, Inc.

151 West 26th Street, floor 3
New York, NY 10001-6810
212 243 3434 fax 212 243 3586

the creative firm of
Two Twelve Associates
New York, New York
with real-life designer
Lisa Mooney
created this business card for
PWA · LTI

Long straight lines of this short card are balanced by green
and blue circles and curves in the logos.

the creative firm of
Anstey Healy Design
Portland, Oregon
with real-life designers
Abigail Anstey & Catherine Healy
created this business card for
Island Kine

Business card accentuates location with aerial drawing
of the Hawaiian Islands and tropical artwork.

Carol Hull
P.O. Box 257
Hermiston, Oregon 97838
(541) 567-3334 FAX 567-4763
~
P.O. Box 2186
Pearl City, Hawaii 96782

the creative firm of
Direction Design
Los Angeles, California
with real-life creative director & designer
Anja Mueller

The rich colors chosen for this series of cards is notable. Consistent fronts employ a golden yellow while card backs are printed with various shades. Spotty halftone texture, which translates into the logo house, is repeated on card backs even larger.

Indian Rock Imagesetting

(510) 843-8973

Mark Hagar

2115 Fourth Street
Berkeley, California 94710
fax (510) 843-4991
data (510) 843-1527
www.indianrock.com

professional digital imaging & prepress

the creative firm of
Fifth Street Design
Berkeley, California
with real-life partners
J. Clifton Meek & Brenton Beck
created this business card for
Indian Rock Imagesetting

Nodding at dots-per-inch technology, small squares dance across the logo of this digital imaging and prepress company. Rainbow-colored dots appear cubelike with dimensionality created by modeling and shadow use.

the creative firm of
David Carter Design Assoc.
Dallas, Texas
with real-life designers
Sharon LeJeune & Randall Hill
created this business card for
Dani

Oddly-angled edge on folded card suggests an upbeat atmosphere for SeventeenSeventeen Restaurant. A delightful mix of fonts in various colors completes the feeling of vitality.

Kent Rathbun
corporate executive chef & general manager

• • •

telephone 214.444.9792 ext. 18   pager 214.848.3511
facsimile 214.444.0990   mobile 214.704.0907
chef@dani1717.com   www.dani1717.com
2156 west northwest highway   suite 311   dallas, texas 75220

SEVENTEEN SEVENTEEN
RESTAURANT

world class cuisine

the creative firm of
Strong Productions
Cedar Rapids, Iowa
with real-life designers
Brian Cox, Matt Doty, & Todd Schatzberg
created this business card for
Paleobiological Fund

Earthy green is printed in blocks of different percentages. Fossils encircled by connecting lines indicate how all live things (or once-live things) are connected.

The Paleobiological Fund

Headquarters:
P. O. Box 526
North Liberty, IA 52317

Phone: 319-626-4062
Email: cpaleo@aol.com
http://members.aol.com/cpaleo

the creative firm of
Kendra Power Design & Communication
Pittsburgh, Pennsylvania
with real-life designer
Kathy Kendra
created this business card for
J.A. Lott Design & Associates

Stock with a muted, checkered background was a perfect choice for this card. The initial logo repeats the shapes as it is built from blocks in stronger colors.

Jill Marcus Balmuth
Designer & Vice President

J.A. LOTT DESIGN & ASSOCIATES

1275 Murray Hill Avenue
Pittsburgh, PA 15217.1216
Phone 412.421.9330
Fax 412.421.9334

Care Facilities   Hospitality   Interior Design   Space Planning

PIECE WORK
PRODUCTIONS

RAY LASKOWITZ
PHOTOGRAPHER
DALLAS, TEXAS
75214-0734

214-941-3678
PWork1121@AOL.com

the creative firm of
Sibley/Peteet Design
Dallas, Texas
with real-life designer
Donna Aldridge
created this business card for
Ray Laskowitz

Almost Cubistic logo is rendered from a camera which has been
dissected and its parts moved. Partial frame leaves an open corner
suggesting a certain amount of freedom in this photographer's work.

the creative firm of
Maremar, Inc.
Bayamón, Puerto Rico
with real-life designer
Marina Rivón
created this business card for
Maremar, Inc. Graphic Design Studio

Nonobjective image in logo background has an almost
limitless interpretation. One thing is for sure: it is movement
with an artistic flair.

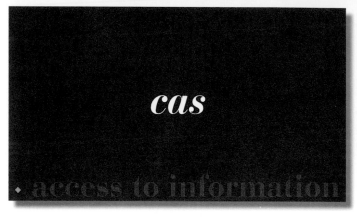

the creative firm of
Fifth Street Design
Berkeley, California
with real-life partners
J. Clifton Meek & Brenton Beck
created this business card for
Computer Access Systems

Beginning with a black box, a visual path is easily followed with the aid of other boxes in different percentages of black. Ending with a white diamond effects an upbeat conclusion.

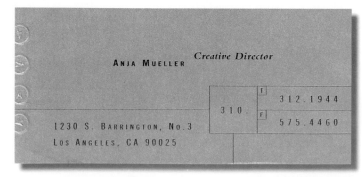

the creative firm of
Direction Design
Los Angeles, California
with real-life creative director & designer
Anja Mueller
created this business card for
Direction Design

This card for Direction Design is full of directional graphics: compasses, long lines, arrows, and blind embossing off the card edge. One side highlights the company and its business. On the other one finds the specifics...name, address, and numbers.

the creative firm of
Trickett & Webb Ltd
London, England
with real-life designers
Lynn Trickett, Brian Webb, & Marcus Taylor
created this business card for
Peter Beavis

Very sturdy business card is printed on flexible plastic. Figure from card back is ethereally visible from the front.

the creative firm of
Visible Ink
Oakland, California
with real-life designer
Sharon Constant
created this business card for
Spider Design

Internet and web site design specialists' logo includes a Black Widow spinning its web over the entire world. Name of company is nicely integrated into the logo by following the circular lines of the globe.

s c h w a

digital design

schwa > 314 621 4141 *fax* 621 3767 *web* http://www.schwa.com/
1307 washington avenue suite 1000-A saint louis missouri 63103

ERIC COSTELLO

e-mail eric@schwa.com

the creative firm of
Phoenix Creative, St. Louis
St. Louis, Missouri
with real-life designers
Steve Wienke & Eric Thoelke
created this business card for
Schwa Digital Design

Bright green, single rounded corner, and (uh) business name
are all unusual and well-related.

CAROL BOBOLTS

RED HERRING DESIGN | 449 WASHINGTON STREET | NYC | 10013

212 219 0557 | FAX 212 219 0720

the creative firm of
Red Herring Design
New York, New York
with real-life designers
Carol Bobolts & Deb Schuler
created this business card for
Red Herring Design

Logo is saved from geometrical symmetry as last initial letter
breaks the visual boundary. Green, radial gradient is printed in
reverse on opposite sides of card.

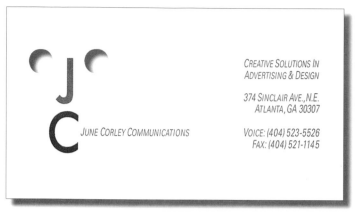

the creative firm of
June Corley Communications
Atlanta, Georgia
with real-life designer
June Corley
created this business card for
June Corley Communications

Comical face is depicted with designer's initials and two die cut eyes.

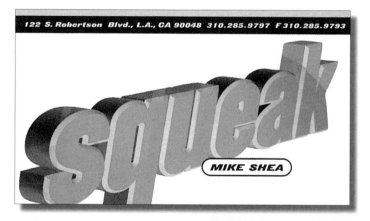

the creative firm of
BRD Design
Hollywood, California
with real-life designer
Peter King Robbins
created this business card for
Squeak Pictures, Inc.

The most notable thing about this card, besides the bright green, is the dimensionality of the logo which translates into a company of solidity.

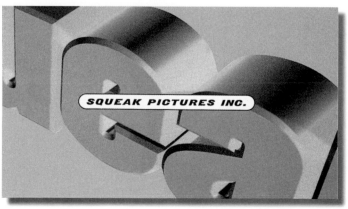

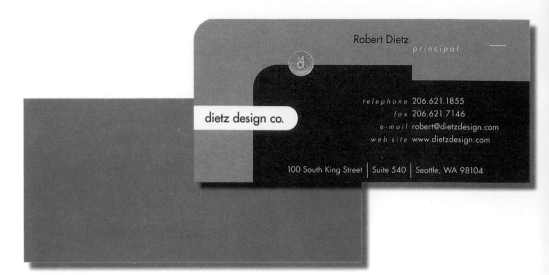

the creative firm of
Dietz Design Co.
Seattle, Washington
with real-life designers
Robert Dietz & Kristie Severn
created this business card for
Dietz Design Co.

Well-constructed design of this business card incudes repeated curves and overlapping shapes. Embossed, foil-stamped initial complements flat inks. Flip side is unexpected bittersweet orange.

the creative firm of
Solutions By Design
Fresno, California
with real-life designer
Scott Wong
created this business card for
Amato

Distinctive dentist's card is strong in design and displays silver-foil stamping. Though unusual in the industry, it maintains a professional image for the cardholder.

the creative firm of
Julia Tam Design
Palos Verdes, California
created this business card for
Jane Brown Interiors

Beautiful logo achieved with the union of script initials is embossed
and gold-foil stamped on this interior designer's business card.

the creative firm of
Visible Ink
Oakland, California
with real-life designer
Sharon Constant
created this business card for
Constant & Frank

Muted hues keep this business card from
becoming too busy. Abstract, pixelated
image is printed in the strongest colors.
Nice script initials of this marketing firm
float across the card's background.

Constant & Frank
Marketing that means business

Sharon Constant
Principal

TEL (510) 836-4845
FAX (510) 836-4846

Higgins House in Preservation Park
678 13th Street, Suite 202
Oakland, CA 94612

*Makers of
Marketing Materials
that Mean Business*

COPYWRITING

GRAPHIC DESIGN

DIRECT MAIL

ADVERTISING CAMPAIGNS

the creative firm of
Schafer
Oakbrook Terrace, Illinois
with real-life designer
Brian Priest
created this business card for
Schafer

Clean design combines the right amount
of arcs and straight lines—all in black
and white.

Samuel P. Sawan, Ph.D.
President

One Industrial Way
Tyngsborough, Massachusetts
01879 USA

T / 978.649.6642 x 11
samsawan@surfacine.com
F / 978.649.4709

www.surfacine.com

the creative firm of
Phoenix Creative, St. Louis
St. Louis, Missouri
with real-life designer
Ed Mantels-Seeker
created this business card for
Monsanto Company/Nidus Center

Blind embossing and foil stamping adds individuality to an
otherwise common card.

GAIL SMITH TIEKEN

TIEKEN DESIGN & CREATIVE SERVICES
3838 North Central Avenue, Suite 100 • Phoenix, Arizona 85012
TEL 602.230.0060 • FAX 602.230.7574
team@tiekendesign.com • www.tiekendesign.com

the creative firm of
Tieken Design & Creative Services
Phoenix, Arizona
with real-life designers
Fred E. Tieken & Rik Boberg
created this business card for
Tieken Design & Creative Services

A portrait of creative ideas, calligraphic, sketchy logo is embossed
and "backwashed" with gray.

the creative firm of
Steve Trapero Design
Silver Spring, Maryland
created this business card for
Cal Pack

Dominant initial cap balances this business card's typography
while serving as a focal point.

CAL PACK

Marc S. Kahn

2424 Mohawk, Suite 12 ~ Pasadena, California 91107 ~ (818)795-8144

the creative firm of
**Phoenix Creative,
St. Louis**
St. Louis, Missouri
with real-life designer
Kathy Wilkinson
created this business card for
Pangaëa/Kelty Pack, Inc.

Squarish card for a company that sells luggage to the economy traveler is printed in earthy greens, black, and a spot of red. Back of card offers a definition of the business name which, all of a sudden, makes the earth seem smaller.

PANGAËA BY KELTY

6235 LOOKOUT ROAD

BOULDER, COLORADO 80301

1-888-558-9726 : EXT 3117

TOM KNOLL
SALES COORDINATOR

FAX NO. : 1-800-504-2745

e-mail: tom@pangaea-travel.com

WWW.PANGAEA-TRAVEL.COM

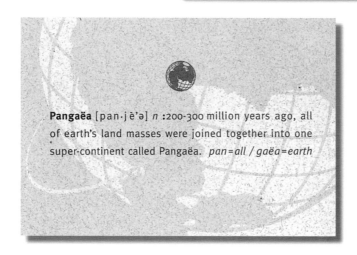

Pangaëa [pan·j ë'ə] *n* :200-300 million years ago, all of earth's land masses were joined together into one super-continent called Pangaëa. *pan=all / gaëa=earth*

RICK W. LEVI   PRESIDENT

CONSOLIDATED
CORRECTIONAL
FOODSERVICE

2894 106th St. | Suite 104 | Des Moines, IA 50322

(515) 278-9774 | Fax (515) 254-0394

A DIVISION OF CONSOLIDATED MANAGEMENT CO.

the creative firm of
Sayles Graphic Design
Des Moines, Iowa
created this business card for
Consolidated Management Co.

Without getting too serious, this card hints strongly at its clientele with bars and stenciled-style typography. The business is a correctional institutions food service.

the creative firm of
Phoenix Creative, St. Louis
St. Louis, Missouri
with real-life designer
Deborah Finkelstein
created this business card for
Kaldis Coffee Roasting

Atypical mix of centered, flush left, and flush right text balances well. Tall, narrow letters in the name of this coffee roaster / coffee house & wholesaler suggests the freespiritedness often associated with such a business.

the creative firm of
Sayles Graphic Design
Des Moines, Iowa
with real-life designer
John Sayles
created this business card for
McArthur Companies

Whimsical illustration with handwritten letters are a visual expression of this company's name whose business is lawn care products.

the creative firm of
Shields Design
Fresno, California
created this business card for
Main Street Trading Company

Main Street Trading Company is found where Main and Wall Street intersect, metaphorically speaking. Illustrative logo integrates crosshatching and gradients, hand- and computer-drawing techniques (though I imagine it was all done on the computer).

Micky Dillon
PRESIDENT

96 Corporate Park
Suite 210
Irvine, CA 92714
714-756-8254
Fax 714-756-1416

the creative firm of
Hornall Anderson Design Works
Seattle, Washington
with real-life designers
Jack Anderson, Scott Eggers, Leo Raymundo
created this business card for
Mahlum & Nordfors

Business card that informs the viewer of a merger between two companies has a perforated tear-off with the names of the individual businesses. After a specified date, the corner is to be detached; the new firm's card remains.

McKINLEY GORDON

MAHLUM & NORDFORS

before May 10, 1993

after May 10, 1993

MAHLUM & NORDFORS McKINLEY GORDON

GARY L. SIGNS, AIA

2505 Third Avenue, Suite 219
Seattle, Washington 98121
(206) 441-4151
(206) 441-0478 fax

Cary S. Collins
Principal

Collins and Associates
Post Office Box 192955
San Francisco, California 9411 9
tel. 415 695 0830
fax. 415 826 7392

the creative firm of
Oh Boy, A Design Company
San Francisco, California
with real-life designer
David Salanitro
created this business card for
Collins & Associates

Business card for accountants is more creative than most in this field.
Corners are rounded with the information reversed out of full bleed
brown ink. A touch of humor is added with a small cartoon hand
pushing numbers in the zip code.

the creative firm of
DAM Creative
Dallas, Texas
with real-life designer
Mark K. Platt
created this business card for
Whole Bean Creative

Great coffee cup ring decorates the background as it plays
off the business name.

the creative firm of
Oh Boy, A Design Company
San Francisco, California
with real-life designers
Alice Chang, David Salanitro
created these business cards for
Novo Interactive

Internet marketer's cards are printed with different
photographic artwork. Each image is within a screen and
partially blurred indicating action.

Digital Commerce Architects

novo interactive

---

222 Sutter Street, Sixth Floor San Francisco, California 94108
t 415 646 7099 f 415 646 7001 www.novointeractive.com

Alicia Astrich, Account Director
alicia@novointeractive.com

novo interactive

Digital Commerce Architects

novo interactive

Digital Commerce Architects

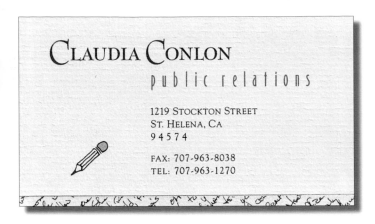

the creative firm of
Buttitta Design
Healdsburg, California
created this business card for
Claudia Conlon

Friendly-looking card uses lightweight fonts, soft colors, drawn pencil,
and a border devised from handwritten text.

the creative firm of
Mires Design, Inc.
San Diego, California
created this business card for
Moore and Associates

Card for corporate search consultants (head hunters) exudes a
strength with dark colors and hard edges, but is not threatening
because of limited script font use and curved lines within boxes.

the creative firm of
Adkins/Balchunas
Providence, Rhode Island
with real-life designer
Jerry Balchunas
created this business card for
London Lennie's

Soft gradient is printed full bleed in the background. It
incorporates hues found in stronger shades in the logo.

A TRADITION OF QUALITY FOR THE NEXT MILLENIUM
LONDON
Our 40th
LENNIE'S

Barry Frommer
General Manager

63-88 Woodhaven Blvd.
Rego Park, NY 11374
Tel 718-894-8084
Fax 718-894-5258
barry@londonlennies.com

belyea.

Patricia Belyea
PRINCIPAL

patricia@belyea.com

1250 Tower Building
1809 Seventh Avenue
Seattle, WA 98101

206.682.4895
FAX 206.623.8912
WEB belyea.com

marketing

communication

design

the creative firm of
Belyea
Seattle, Washington
with real-life art director
Patricia Belyea
and designer
Ron Lars Hansen
created this business card for
Belyea

Two sides of this design firm are
exemplified on the two sides of its
business card. One side is more
traditionally corporate: clean lines,
repeated shapes in a play on negative
space. The other side shows the artistry
they offer with bright orange and
painterly effects.

the creative firm of
Kevin Akers—Designer
San Rafael, California
with real-life designer
Kevin Akers
created this personal card for
Suzanne & Doug Kline

Golden yellow and maroon look well together, but are different enough in tone to work as definers as they are used in completely separate capacities. Beautiful illustration of (one assumes) the Kline's home is a perfect background for this personal card.

the creative firm of
Phoenix Creative, St. Louis
St. Louis, Missouri
with real-life designer
Ed Mantels-Seeker
created this business card for
Mitchell and Hugeback

Lines form an architecturally-styled drawing as the logo. Fine lines and boxes are repeated on card front and back.

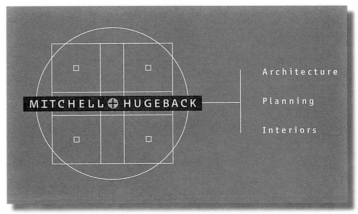

Ora J. Williamson
Executive Director, Market Development
orajean@conversa.com

cǫnversā

conversational
computing

9891 S. Atherton Way
Highlands Ranch, CO 8 0 1 2 6
303.683.6490 F 303.683.6574

the creative firm of
**Hornall Anderson
Design Works**
Seattle, Washington
with real-life designers
**Jack Anderson, Kathy Saito,
& Alan Copeland**
created these business cards for
Conversá

Conversa employs a dialogue balloon for the O in its logo
name. Card backs are printed full bleed in either bold red or
yellow.

BRIAN BENNETT
National Sales Manager
303.530.7670 ext.3113

THE FIRST NAME IN BACKPACKING

6235 Lookout Road Boulder, Colorado 80301
fax 800.504.2745 www.kelty.com bbennett@kelty.com

the creative firm of
Phoenix Creative, St. Louis
St. Louis, Missouri
with real-life designer
Deborah Finkelstein
created this business card for
Kelty Pack, Inc.

Utilizing a photographic rendering of its product label on this
card is a good way to consistently use the company logo,
familiarizing the public with its corporate identity.

83 COLUMBIA ST. SUITE 400, SEATTLE, WA 98104

TEL 206·682·3685   FAX 206·682·3867

HAMMERQUIST & HALVERSON

KAY WOOD

E-MAIL kay@hammerquist.net

the creative firm of
Hornall Anderson Design Works
Seattle, Washington
with real-life designers
Jack Anderson & Mike Calkins
created these business cards for
Hammerquist & Halverson

Lots of out-of-the-ordinary techniques are used on these cards.
A yellow paw print is thermograved on card front (notice the
bullseye). Metallic silver ink is printed with a three-sided bleed;
text is reversed out of this and also printed on it. Corners are
rounded on the card that is slightly taller and narrower than usual.
Finally, printed full bleed on the back are two monochromatic
photos, one a bulldog's face, the other a dart board bullseye
(remember the logo?).

the creative firm of
Margo Chase Design
Los Angeles, California
created this business card for
Margo Chase Design

Target audience of this graphic design studio is obviously multicultural. Nice way to handle the language difference is to print one on one side, the other on the other.

margo chase design
2255 bancroft avenue
los angeles, ca 90039 usa
tel:213.668.1055 fax:213.668.2470

MARGO CHASE

マーゴ チェイス デザイン
ロスアンゼルス市バンクロフトアベニュー2255
電話：213.668.1055　ファックス：213.668.2470

the creative firm of
Z•D Studios, Inc.
Madison, Wisconsin
with real-life designer
Mark Schmitz
created this business card for
Pop Pictures

"Pop" is the business name and that's just what this card does. Large in size, it's printed with bright colors and bold graphics. Notice that even though there's no extra space between names, color use separates them.

POP
PICTURES
DAVID**FLEER**

1501 Monroe Street
Madison WI 53711-2020
phone:608.256.35MM
fax:608.259.0559

the creative firm of
Hornall Anderson Design Works
Seattle, Washington
with real-life designers
Jack Anderson, Belinda Bowling,
Andrew Smith, & Ed Lee
created this business card for
Streamworks

This business card resembles an address label or even a ticket. Initial logo is printed in a manner that appears as if it is stamped in the background.

the creative firm of
Janet Payne Graphic Designer
Hopewell, New Jersey
with real-life designer
Janet Payne
created this business card for
Mary L. Harrison

Appropriately, the border around all pertinent information on this wedding and event consultant's card looks like a party.

PROMOTIONS

SPECIAL EVENTS

CORPORATE IDENTITY

PUBLIC SERVICE

NOT-FOR-PROFIT n

COMMUNITY HEALTH c

CHILDREN'S ISSUES

At the **Av**... great compo... commitment to...

serv... **Public R**... organizations so...

Avrin Public Relations Group pro... ...help improve the health of our community. We work closely with other advocacy organizations to provide educational materials and promote pub... As the director of the Colorado Chapter... closely with M... youn...

PUBLIC RELATIONS

PRODUCTS • SERVICES • MESSAGE

AVRIN
public relations group

IDENTITY

p

POSITIONING

STORY PLACEMENT

MEDIA TRAINING

MEDIA RELATIONS

TELEVISION • RADIO • PRINT

AVRIN
public relations group

INTERNET

m

DAVID L. AVRIN
PRESIDENT

PH: 303.795.9898
FX: 303.795.8880
PAGER: 303.890.8097
E-MAIL: AvrinPR@aol.com

AVRIN
public relations group

SG PLAZA | 2305 E. ARAPAHOE ROAD | SUITE 201 | LITTLETON | COLORADO 80122

the creative firm of
**X Design
Company**
Littleton, Colorado
with real-life designer
Alex Valderrama
created these business cards for
Avrin Public Relations

A normal-sized business card just couldn't accommodate all the information this public relations firm wanted to disseminate. Each of the larger cards focuses on a single aspect of the company's business.

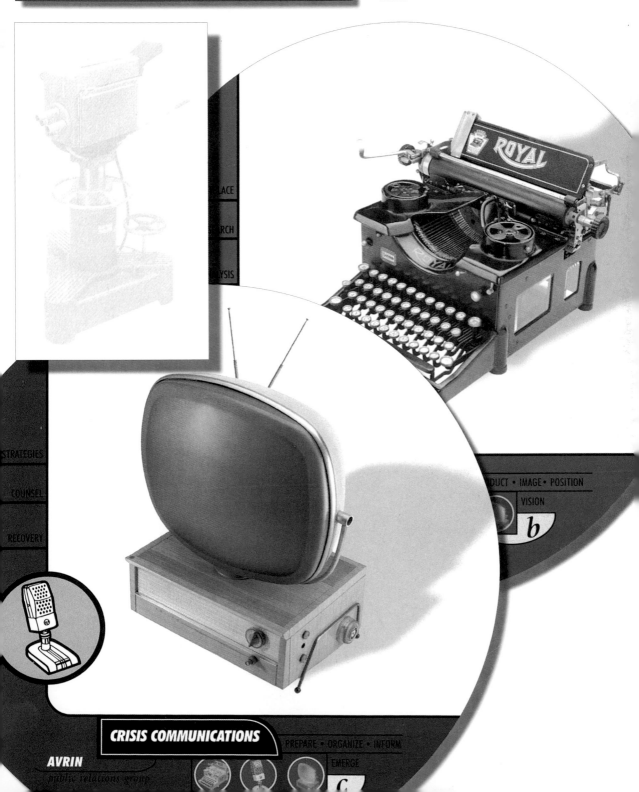

ELAINE TALLIA

ASSISTANT MANAGER

8400 SANTA MONICA BLVD.

WEST HOLLYWOOD,

CALIFORNIA 90069

FAX 213.848.9447

TELEPHONE 213.848.2360

the creative firm of
Vrontikis Design Office
Los Angeles, California
created this business card for
Cafe La Bohème

Eclectic typography speaks to the name of this
upscale international restaurant. Angled geometric
shapes all relate on a grid.

GERRY KEARBY
Founder & CEO
415.562.0886
kearby@liquidaudio.com

LIQUID AUDIO

2421 Broadway Second Floor Redwood City CA 94063 FAX 562.0899 www.liquidaudio.com

the creative firm of
Cooksherman
San Francisco, California
with real-life designers
Ken Cook & Inka Mulia
created this business card for
Liquid Audio

Color from embossed and foil
stamped logo is printed full bleed
on card back. Curve from audio
swirl is repeated in card top and
bottom edges.

PHONE 630.365.2640
PAGE 888.360.2990

the creative firm of
Z•D Studios, Inc.
Madison, Wisconsin
with real-life designer
Mark Schmitz
created this business card for
Peich

Really interesting typographical treatments are used on this card. Name of business is handwritten in the background, printed in sans serif in foreground, and shadowed in a rubber stamp font. Name and title, address, and numbers are all set at differing angles, one of which is mimicked with an unexpected edge cut.

MARILYN STUBBLEFIELD *Case Manager, Specializing in Support Services*

BIG BROTHERS BIG SISTERS OF GREATER ST. LOUIS
4625 Lindell Blvd Suite 501 St. Louis, MO 63108 **314-361-5900 ext 14** fax 314-361-4484

the creative firm of
Phoenix Creative, St. Louis
St. Louis, Missouri
with real-life designer
Deborah Finkelstein
created this business card for
Big Brothers Big Sisters of Greater St. Louis

This card appears to be designed with two different audiences in mind—much like the Big Brothers Big Sisters program itself. One side is more traditional, straight-on in its message, sure to appeal to the parents involved. The flip side, which is printed with the motto of the group, is looser and less rigidly designed which surely speaks to a freer-thinking set, the kids.

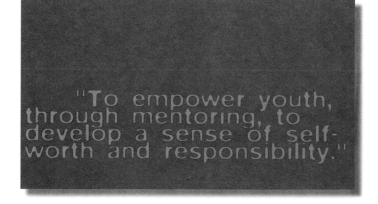

"To empower youth, through mentoring, to develop a sense of self-worth and responsibility."

the creative firm of
Greg Welsh Design
Seattle, Washington
created this business card for
Swiss Skin Care Clinique

Large, halftoned female face printed in the background is gold foil stamped over with company logo. Foil stamping at card bottom follows the curve from the orbiting Cs in the initial logo.

S w i s s   S k i n   C a r e   C l i n i q u e

Lorilee Sandusky
European trained
Esthetician

206.746.0440

13401 Bel-Red Road Suite B-12 Bellevue, WA 98005

Cigar	Sunroser	Shibuya-Ku		FAX:
	Daikanyama	Tokyo	TEL:	03
Wine &	B1F	150	03	5489
	11-6		5489	2506
Jazz Club	Sarugaku		2202	
	Cho	WWW.GLOBAL-DINING.COM		

葉巻	サンローゼ	渋谷区		FAX:
	代官山	東京	TEL:	03
ワイン	B1F	150	03	5489
	11-6		5489	2506
ジャズクラブ	猿楽町		2202	
		WWW.GLOBAL-DINING.COM		

the creative firm of
Vrontikis Design Office
Los Angeles, California
created this business card for
Tableaux Lounge

Cigar, wine, and jazz club, located in Tokyo, has a strong American appeal so the business card must be printed in both Japanese and English as it is done here on opposite sides.

MICHELLE
LANTING

CERTIFIED
MASSAGE
THERAPIST

SWEDISH-ESALEN
REFLEXOLOGY

*JUST AS POTTERS TEMPER CLAY,
SO MASSAGE TEMPERS THE BODY*

4721
GUENZA RD.
SANTA ROSA
CA 95404
707 571 8777

the creative firm of
Buttitta Design
Healdsburg, California
created this business card for
Michelle Lanting

Abstract hands printed softly in the background on this massage therapist's card complement the sensuality of the smooth curves of the left border.

Anu Mahal
International Sales Director

Suissa International Beauty Co.
440 Rumsey Ct.   San Jose, CA 95111   USA
Ph: +1.408.365.7867   Fax: +1.408.972.2600
EMail: amahal@aol.com

the creative firm of
Kevin Akers—Designer
San Rafael, California
with real-life designer
Kevin Akers
created this business card for
Suissa Beauty Co.

The Swiss are known for their clean design as is demonstrated in the initials found in this logo for a beauty supplier. International company's tagline is reversed out of metallic gold on card back.

World Beauty for

Body and Soul

the creative firm of
Hoffmann & Angelic Design
Surrey, (BC) Canada
with real-life designers
Andrea Hoffmann & Ivan Angelic
created this business card for
To Market To Market

Text on a gently flowing path leads the viewer's eye To Market. Stroked logo indicates freedom and movement for this company that sells products on the Internet.

the creative firm of
Ed Mantels-Seeker
St. Louis, Missouri
with real-life designer
Ed Mantels-Seeker
created this business card for
Hawkins & DeLear

Feminist folk musicians' card has fresh colors and square shape with an unexpected orientation.

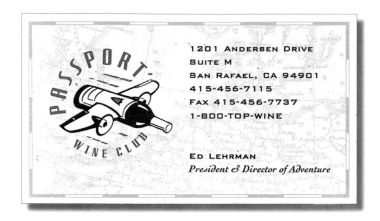

the creative firm of
Kevin Akers—Designer
San Rafael, California
with real-life designer
Kevin Akers
created this business card for
Passport Wine Club

Wine-of-the-month club really delivers with a jet body that is a wine bottle. Background of card is printed with a muted map which indicates the internationality of the wines offered.

the creative firm of
Cathey Associates
Dallas, Texas
with real-life designer
Isabel Campos
created this business card for
Jwana Juice

Illustrative logo suggests the business of this juice bar. Back of card is printed with a legendary account of how the company came to be. (The name isn't Swahili. Ask it out loud...)

The Jwana Story

On a lush, tropical island in a far away corner of the world — where the seas are always smooth and the fruit trees grow to the sky — there is a very tall, snowcapped mountain called Mount Jwana. There, icy waters from the slopes above cascade into the valleys below blending with the sweet nectar and juices of the island's amazing variety of fresh fruits and vegetables. The very happy islanders call these deliciously fresh and nutritious natural blends Jwana Juice.

An island myth says that Jwana Juice tastes so good it makes iguanas smile.

the creative firm of
AERIAL
San Francisco, California
with real-life designer
Tracy Moon
created this business card for
violet.com

Many out-of-the-ordinary techniques are used in the design of this business card for an online boutique, but most noticeable is the designer's resistance to temptation to make the ink color equivalent to the business name.

www.violet.com

violet
anything but ordinary gifts

4104 24th street   no. 415
san francisco 94114
tel 415.285.3573
fax 415.285.3563

violet@violet.com
www.violet.com

GARY MUSZYNSKI
Program Director
ONE WORLD MUSIC
524 Trinity Avenue
St. Louis, Missouri 63130
314 863-2007
314 863-3355 Facsimile

the creative firm of
Ed Mantels-Seeker
St. Louis, Missouri
with real-life designer
Ed Mantels-Seeker
created this business card for
One World Music

Exactly how a samba-based employee-motivation program works has yet to be experienced by me; I do know that music is a unifier that crosses many barriers, hence the business name.

NAOMI EIGNER
Program Coordinator
ONE WORLD MUSIC
524 Trinity Avenue
St. Louis, Missouri 63130
314 863-2007
314 863-3355 Facsimile

the creative firm of
Phoenix Creative, St. Louis
St. Louis, Missouri
with real-life designer
Ed Mantels-Seeker
created this business card for
Carlos Mindreau

Minimalist card for an architect is built with fine lines, dotted lines, and curves.

the creative firm of
Sandy Gin Design
Palo Alto, California
with real-life designer
Sandy Gin
created this business card for
Sandy Gin Design

Wedge-shaped card's type is reversed out of a black background. A head with abstract facial features formed from initials of the designer is the logo.

the creative firm of
Adkins/Balchunas
Providence, Rhode Island
with real-life designers
**Susan DeAngelis
& Jerry Balchunas**
created this business card for
Harvest Moon

Everything about this business card
suggests a naturalness. Earthy tones,
agricultural photo, and company name
well befit the image of a restaurant that
also offers prepared take-home meals.

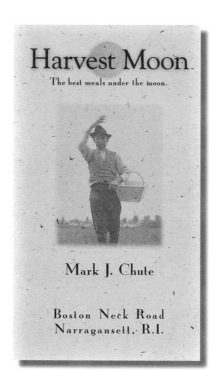

the creative firm of
Phoenix Creative, St. Louis
St. Louis, Missouri
with real-life designer
Deborah Finkelstein
created this business card for
Anneibur Creations

Having stickers, as opposed to business cards, printed allows
multitudinous freedom with application. They can be used for
address labels, attached to business cards, put on
merchandise...

the creative firm of
Hornall Anderson Design Works
Seattle, Washington
with real-life designers
Jack Anderson, Mary Hermes, & Leo Raymundo
created this business card for
Watson Furniture Company

Stylized W is easily read. Distinction to card is added by rounded
and square opposite corners.

the creative firm of
Phoenix Creative, St. Louis
St. Louis, Missouri
with real-life designer
Ed Mantels-Seeker
created this membership card for
Saint Louis Heroes

Fat card is presented to those who support the city improvement efforts of St. Louis 2004.

the creative firm of

Hornall Anderson
Design Works
Seattle, Washington
with real-life designers
Jack Anderson, Heidi Favour,
Mary Chin Hutchison,
& Bruce Branson-Meyer
created these business cards for
Print NW/Six Sigma

Each card in this series is identical in design
to the others with the exception of color
choice which is used with black, and
reversed white text.

Plant Address:

Pager (in OR)   4918 20th Street East   Pager (in WA)
503.499.8282   Fife, WA 98424   206.552.6087
            Mobile: 503.781.4787

PRINT

5200 Southwest Macadam, Suite 535, Portland, OR 97201
503.242.1474 or 503.242.2339
Plant: 1.800.451.5742   Fax: 1.503.242.2550

PRINT NW   SIX SIGMA

DIANA BRADBURY
Regional Sales Manager

5200 Southwest Macadam, Suite 535, Portland, OR 97201
503.242.1474 or 503.242.2339
Plant: 1.800.451.5742   Fax: 1.503.242.2550

PRINT NW   SIX SIGMA

KAREN PATRICELLI
Marketing Manager

P.O. Box 1418, Tacoma, WA 98401
206.922.9393 1.800.451.5742
Fax: 1.206.922.3383

PRINT NW   SIX SIGMA

DIANA BRADBURY
Regional Sales Manager

5200 Southwest Macadam, Suite 535, Portland, OR 97201
503.242.1474 or 503.242.2339
Plant: 1.800.451.5742   Fax: 1.503.242.2550

the creative firm of
Kevin Akers—Designer
San Rafael, California
with real-life designer
Kevin Akers
created this business card for
Susan Sargent Designs

Textured stock complements rough-edged logo. Notice that enlarged version of the logo is printed is a differing color scheme than the one with text.

the creative firm of
Phoenix Creative, St. Louis
St. Louis, Missouri
with real-life designer
Ed Mantels-Seeker
created this business card for
Simply Cruises

Colorful iconography is presented in almost a gesture-drawing format. Excellent choice of inks match the "confetti" in the card stock.

the creative firm of
Phoenix Creative, St. Louis
St. Louis, Missouri
with real-life designer
Ed Mantels-Seeker
created this business card for
David R. Francis Society

Traditional design includes a photo of David R. Francis, the man for whom this society is named. Flip side of card has dates screened out of full bleed gold, indicating the group not only keeps its eyes on its past but future as well.

Amy H. Whitelaw

THE DAVID R. FRANCIS SOCIETY

Post Office Box 16656
St. Louis, Missouri 63105
314 991-3301 Telephone
314 991-4257 Facsimile

the creative firm of
X Design Company
Littleton, Colorado
with real-life designer
Alex Valderrama
created this business card for
X Design Company

Bold graphics are printed in strong red, gold, and black. Enlarged logo is screened in the background.

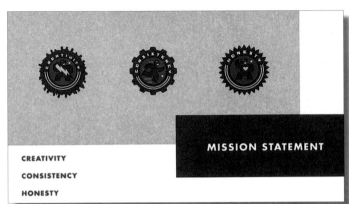

the creative firm of
Sayles Graphic Design
Des Moines, Iowa
with real-life designer
John Sayles
created this business card for
1999 Sayles Graphic Design

Overlapping boxes are found on both sides of card. One offers address information and other vital statistics. The flip side is printed with a simple mission statement using an iconic family of logos.

the creative firm of
Gee + Chung Design
San Francisco, California
with real-life art director
Earl Gee
and designers
Earl Gee & Fani Chung
created this business card for
Alliance Healthcare Foundation

This card becomes very individualized with sides angled interiorly. Look closely and you can see this shape in the logo several times.

111

the creative firm of
Kevin Akers—Designer
San Rafael, California
with real-life designer
Kevin Akers
created this business card for
Marilyn Bennett

Business card for a photo stylist has a lot of illustrative style itself.
Shades of pink and a consistent theme of "hands-on" relate the front
and back of card.

the creative firm of
Kiku Obata & Company
St. Louis, Missouri
with real-life designer
Ed Mantels-Seeker
created this business card for
The Vein Center

Beautiful color execution almost makes the
viewer forget of what the purple is indicative.

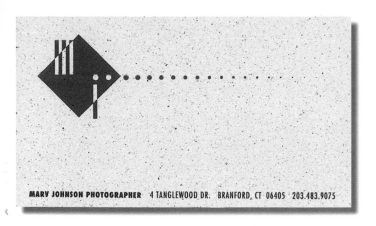

MARV JOHNSON PHOTOGRAPHER   4 TANGLEWOOD DR.   BRANFORD, CT 06405   203.483.9075

the creative firm of
Kevin Akers—Designer
San Rafael, California
with real-life designer
Kevin Akers
created this business card for
Marv Johnson

Stylized initial caps redefine the negative and positive space of this photographer's logo.

the creative firm of
After Hours Creative
Phoenix, Arizona
with real-life designers
After Hours Creative
created this business card for
The Cotton Center

Taupe and purple colors create a nice balance. Logo is enlarged and screened on both front and back.

the creative firm of
Sheehan Design
Seattle, Washington
with real-life designer
Jamie Sheehan
created this appointment card for
Pacific Dental Care

Heavy vellum printed with silver metallic ink imitates a dental x-ray on the back of this card.

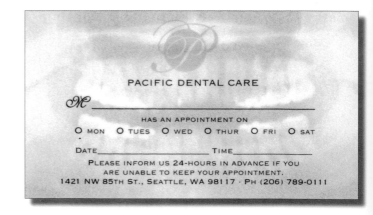

PACIFIC DENTAL CARE

*M*_____

HAS AN APPOINTMENT ON

O MON   O TUES   O WED   O THUR   O FRI   O SAT

DATE_____   TIME_____

PLEASE INFORM US 24-HOURS IN ADVANCE IF YOU
ARE UNABLE TO KEEP YOUR APPOINTMENT.
1421 NW 85TH ST., SEATTLE, WA 98117 · PH (206) 789-0111

Spelman & Associates

**Search Consultants for
the Biotechnology Industry
21 Tamal Vista Blvd. Ste. 200
Corte Madera, CA 94925
[415] 945-1800
fax [415] 945-1888**

Lauren Spelman

the creative firm of
Kevin Akers—Designer
San Rafael, California
with real-life designer
Kevin Akers
created this business card for
Spelman & Associates

Simplified DNA strand is the focus of this logo for search consultants for the biotechnology industry.

CLEARDATA.NET

John Harris
V. P. Finance
5956 Sherry Lane   Dallas, TX 75225
phone 214.750.1599 ext 237
fax 214.750.7086
email john.harris@cleardata.net

the creative firm of
After Hours Creative
Phoenix, Arizona
with real-life designers
After Hours Creative
created this business card for
ClearData.net

Visual play on business name is achieved with the word "clear" die cut from card.

the creative firm of
Vestigio
Sra. Da Hora, Portugal
with real-life designer
Emanuel Barbosa
created this business card for
Latido

Fun typography and cartoon-style drawing keep the bone image upbeat on this card for a pet shop.

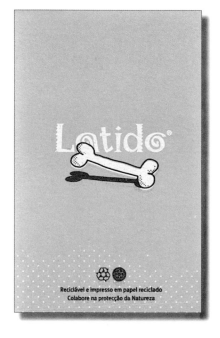

the creative firm of

Hon's Design
Singapore
with real-life designer
Hon Soo Tien
created these business cards for
Hon's Design

Large variety of cards show a vast design capability. This, along with every card not having the same amount of information, allows the designer to choose the most appropriate card for each client or prospective client.

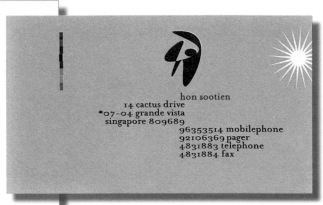

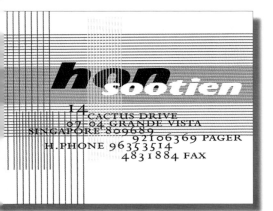

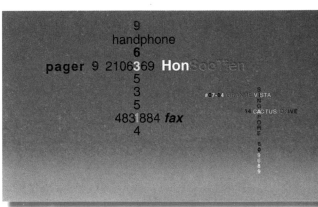

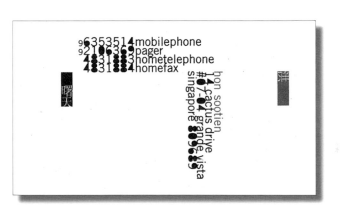

the creative firm of
Oh Boy, A Design Company
San Francisco, California
with real-life designers
Hunter L. Wimmer & David Salanitro
created this business card for
Freestyle Interactive

Pixels in loosely-grouped formation freely interact as they guide the viewer's eye to the company name.

Rand Ragusa
Director of Sales and Marketing
rand@freestylesoft.com

freestyle
interactive

58 Second Street, San Francisco, California 94105
t 415 778 0611 f 415 778 0614 **www.freestylesoft.com**

the creative firm of
Sayles Graphic Design
Des Moines, Iowa
created this business card for
Beckley Imports

This auto repair shop's card depicts its business in a positive light. Plainly not shade-tree mechanics, Beckley Imports does not exude snobbery; it's easy to hit one or the other extreme. Tire track driven across the card is a great touch.

Wild Bill's
Custom Food Company

W. B. Bill Smith
Smoked & Marinated Meats

214-348-1466
bkos @ cmpu.net

the creative firm of
Cathey Associates, Inc.
Dallas, Texas
with real-life designer
Matt Westapher
created this business card for
Wild Bill's

Custom food company that specializes in smoked and marinated meats isn't afraid to let you know its business with a kicking donkey in the logo.

the creative firm of
X Design Company
Littleton, Colorado
with real-life designers
Alex Valderrama & Courtney Burbridge
created this business card for
EventSmiths

Abstract smithy hammers out the business initial in parody of the company name. Heavy black border accents the single rounded corner which is mirrored from the logo.

the creative firm of
Cooksherman
San Francisco, California
with real-life designer
Ken Cook
created this business card for
Andromedia

Calligraphic figure, which utilizes the company initial, is embossed and gold foil stamped on card. Unity is created with logo touching the light and dark card divisions.

JOHANN V. LYNCH *senior software engineer*
johann@andromedia.com

545 Mission St
Second Floor
San Francisco
Calif 94105
415.278.0717
fax.278.0719
www.andromedia.com

ANDROMEDIA

the creative firm of
Tharp Did It
Los Gatos, California
created this card for
Tharp, O'Connor & Heer

Humorous card has an attitude (even if it's thinly-veiled). *I wonder if they get a lot of invitations to dinner...*

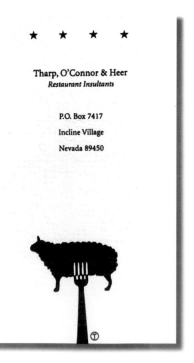

★   ★   ★   ★

Tharp, O'Connor & Heer
Restaurant Insultants

P.O. Box 7417

Incline Village

Nevada 89450

fork ewe!

HOME
P O Box 254
(260 Bean Avenue)
Bodega Bay, CA 94923
707/875-2165

STUDIO
34 Mountain Spring Ave.
San Francisco, CA 94114
415/731-9979
415/753-8955 private
415/566-0306 fax

SUZANNE CUSHMAN &
NOEL BARNHURST

the creative firm of
Kevin Akers—Designer
San Rafael, California
with real-life designer
Kevin Akers
created this personal card for
Suzanne Cushman & Noel Barnhurst

Spot varnish on logo adds a richness to an otherwise perfectly
fine printing job. Home and studio information increases utilization
of the card.

179 SOUTH LAFAYETTE STREET
DENVER | COLORADO | 80209 | USA

1-303-722-3132 tel
1-303-777-5866 fax
1-917-743-2423 cell

LANGLIA 11
0854 OSLO | NORWAY

47-22693337 tel
47-92830135 cell

KIRSTEN KOKKIN
Sculpture Studio

WWW.OPENARTSHOW.COM/KOKKIN | EMAIL: KOKKIN@COMPUSERVE.COM

the creative firm of
X Design Company
Littleton, Colorado
with real-life designer
Alex Valderrama
created this business card for
Kirsten Kokkin

Printed in metallic gold, this logo is implemented with
repeated shapes devised from artist's initials. Card back is a
photo of the sculptor's work.

the creative firm of
Z•D Studios, Inc.
Madison, Wisconsin
with real-life designer
Mark W. Schmitz
created this business card for
Z·D Studios, Inc.

Many companies use initial logos, but not many render them in such a creative format. Die cut and solid triangle produce the Z, while a crescent almost touching the vertical edge of the triangle forms the D. Sphere functions as typographical bullet.

FON   608 257 8400

FAX   608 257 8440

CELL   608 698 6275

EMAIL   ZDOG2@INXPRESS.NET

ZEBRADOG

the creative firm of
Insight Design Communications
Wichita, Kansas
with real-life designer
Chris Parks
created this business card for
Sports Solutions

Yin and yang shapes, almost in the form of a football, are separated by an S garnered from the company name. Good card divisions separate without unrelating different informations: the business and individual's names, and address/phone number information.

the creative firm of
Phoenix Creative, St. Louis
St. Louis, Missouri
with real-life designers
Reid Thompson & Kathy Wilkinson
created this business card for
Firehouse

Somewhat retro design uses overlapping shapes to house information.

the creative firm of
Pfeiffer Plus Company
St. Louis, Missouri
with real-life designer
Todd Doyle
created this business card for
Reprox of St. Louis

Bright, full bleed printing with color code boxes on the card edge almost foregoes the need for words to inform the viewer this is a professional printer's card.

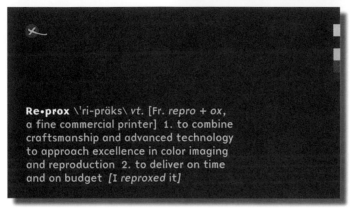

TODD J. KARLIN

408 A BRANCH 92 HIGHWAY
PLATTE CITY, MISSOURI 64079
TEL: (816) 858-5011 • FAX: (816) 858-5360

the creative firm of
EAT Advertising & Design
Kansas City, Missouri
with real-life designers
Paul Prato & Patrice Eilts-Jobe
created this business card for
Karlin & Unger, CPAs

If going to the accountant can be fun, Karlin and Unger must be it. Lighthearted bean-counter artwork sets a very upbeat tone for the firm.

the creative firm of
DeLisle & Associates
Altamonte Springs, Florida
with real-life designer
Michael Ruge
created this business card for
Nightlife Orlando

Interesting image is a black and dark gray sundial used as the background. Broken and askew letters emanate vivacity with a white shadow that effects a glow.

the creative firm of
Supon Design Group
Washington, D.C.
with real-life designer
Supon Phornirunlit & Sharisse Steber
created this business card for
Supon Design Group

Boxes with different illustration techniques and samples adorn the front of this design firm's card.

the creative firm of
SK Designworks Inc.
Philadelphia, Pennsylvania
with real-life designer
Soonduk Krebs
created this business card for
SK Designworks Inc.

Blue collar photographs and mechanical icons are applied within a Constructionist design. Short, wide card's shape is repeated in long text lines and wide black boxes.

the creative firm of
Anstey Healy Design
Portland, Oregon
with real-life designers
Abigail Anstey & Catherine Healy
created this business card for
Anstey Healy Design

Copper foil stamped figure works with colored inks which are found in the paper. The stock is from recycled materials including newsprint. You can actually see tiny pieces of newspaper in the card.

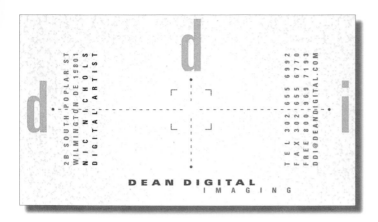

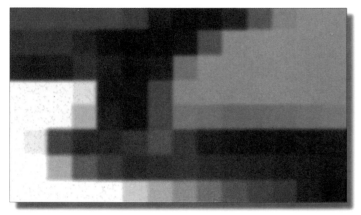

the creative firm of
Michael Gunselman Incorporated
Wilmington, Delaware
with real-life designer
Michael Gunselman
created this business card for
Dean Digital Imaging

An almost perfect balance is formed as the designer divided this card into quadrants. Card back is printed full bleed with a hugely-pixellated image.

the creative firm of
Pinpoint Communications
Deerfield Beach, Florida
with real-life creative director
J. Dudley Davenport
and designer
Stephanie Wikberg
created this business card for
Clark Production Services

Artwork that is a little Cubistic with an almost Socialist theme is a visual metaphor comparing Clark Production to a hard worker, shouldering the responsibility, carrying the weight, getting the job done.

the creative firm of
**Robert Meyers Communication
Design & Planning**
Pittsburgh, Pennsylvania
with real-life designer
Robert Meyers
created these business cards for
Pittsburgh Federation For Events & Promotion

The full bleed photos on the backs of these cards are a real tribute
to the character of the city, showing the best of Pittsburgh.

Kari Carbone
Communications Specialist

~~~

One Riverfront Center
20 Stanwix Street, Suite 300
Pittsburgh, PA 15222-4801

(412) 434-6202
Fax (412) 434-6208

PITTSBURGH
F E D E R A T I O N   F O R
EVENTS &
PROMOTION
Formerly The Pittsburgh Sports & Festival Federation

Daphne Dawn Perry, AIA

Architecture

Interior Design

1255 W. Magnolia

Fort Worth, TX 76104

817·921·0583

the creative firm of
Michael Niblett Design
Fort Worth, Texas
with real-life designer
Michael Niblett
created this business card for
Daphne Dawn Perry, AIA

The logo of this card creates rhythm out of chaos, indicative of the cardholder's profession, architect / interior designer.

the creative firm of
Michael Orr + Associates, Inc.
Corning, New York
with real-life designer
Michael R. Orr
created this business card for
Johnson-Schmidt & Steer Architects

Very distinct statement of style is made with this card. Repetition of blocks and bars hint at the construction side of the architecture field, while the remaining design elements represent aesthetic quality.

ELISE JOHNSON-SCHMIDT
607. 937. 6166
FAX 607. 937. 6137
5 EAST MARKET STREET
SUITE 304
CORNING, NEW YORK 14830

JOHNSON-
SCHMIDT
&
STEER

ARCHITECTS

the creative firm of
Design Services, Inc.
Baton Rouge, Louisiana
with real-life designers
Rod Parker, Chris Steiner, & Nicole Duet
created this business card for
Baton Rouge Gallery

Dark grays printed on deep rust produce an air of mystery,
especially with blurred typography and barren tree artwork.

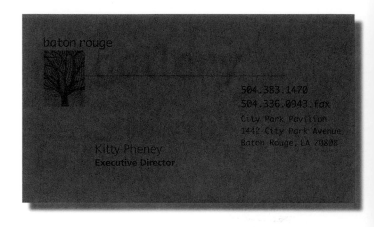

the creative firm of
Hutson San Luis
Monrovia, California
with real-life designer
Roberto San Luis
created this business card for
Hutson San Luis

Folded business card uses monochromatic,
illustrative logo on the cover and inside.

Sarah Swenson
Marketing Communications Associate

Studio Archetype, Inc.
600 Townsend Street
Penthouse
San Francisco, CA 94103
Tel: 415.659.4474
Fax: 415.703.9901
www.studioarchetype.com
sarah@studioarchetype.com

SAN FRANCISCO | NEW YORK | ATLANTA

the creative firm of
Studio Archetype
San Francisco, California
with real-life designers
Clement Mok, Mark Crumpacker,
Grant Peterson, & Andrew Cawrse
created this business card for
Studio Archetype

Business card with clean lines and a typographical concentration
may well be the archetype for a positive identity.

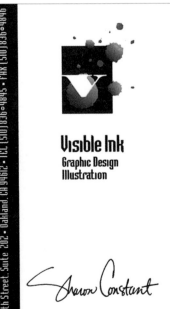

the creative firm of
Visible Ink
Oakland, California
with real-life designer
Sharon Constant
created this business card for
Visible Ink

The opposite of invisible or disappearing ink, this
studio's work apparently makes a lasting statement.

English	Please give me your chef's specialty.
French	S'il vous plaît, donnez moi les spécialités de votre chef.
Hindi	Moojhey app kee weeshaysh cheese deejeeye.
Italian	La specialità della casa, per favore.
Japanese	Itaemae-san no susumehin ga nan desu ka?
Spanish	¡Favor de servirnos la especialidad de la casa!
Thai	Koh sang arai piset kong ranahan nii.

the creative firm of
Belyea
Seattle, Washington
with real-life art director
Patricia Belyea
and designer
Christian Salas
created this business card for
International Dining Adventures

Attention is given to the global aspect of this travel company. Stylized cutlery orbiting the world comprise the logo. On the card back is the phrase "Give me your chef's specialty" in seven different languages.

the creative firm of
A-Hill Design
Albuquerque, New Mexico
with real-life designer
Sandy Hill
created this business card for
Form + Function

Glossy printed stickers adhered to uncoated stock mixes textures, increasing the tactileness of this business card.

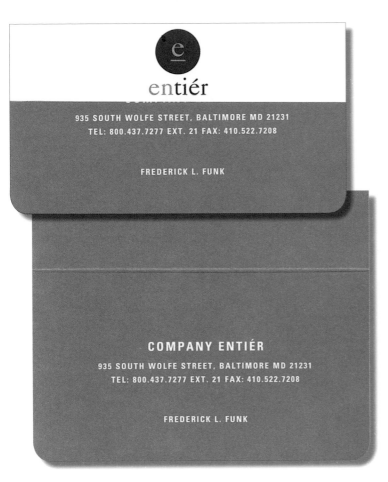

the creative firm of
Gr8
Baltimore, Maryland
with real-life designers
Morton Jackson & Kurt Thesing
created this business card for
Company Entiér

Flap printed with logo lifts to reveal the company's proper name.

Cynthia Thomassey

Child Care, Day Care, Babysitting

286 Brighton Street
East Pittsburgh, PA 15112

412 824-2992

the creative firm of
Seman Design
Pittsburgh, Pennsylvania
with real-life designer
Richard M. Seman
created this business card for
Cynthia Thomassey

Caution sign succeeds in suggesting the cardholder
cares about children—offers child care.

the creative firm of
Randi Wolf Design, Inc.
Glassboro, New Jersey
with real-life designer
Randi Wolf
created this business card for
Randi Wolf Design

Anthropomorphic logo features a picture equivalent to the designer's last name with implement of the trade.

the creative firm of
Sayles Graphic Design
Des Moines, Iowa
with real-life designer
John Sayles
created this business card for
Glazed Expressions

Love the name of this pottery studio! Whimsical artwork echoes the spirit of the company name.

the creative firm of
Phoenix Creative, St. Louis
St. Louis, Missouri
with real-life designer
Deborah Finkelstein
created this business card for
Tangerine

Very appealing name for a lounge/restaurant suggests a fresh atmosphere—probably sweet, a little acrid, and maybe even a bit tart. Typography is all over the place with a charismatic vitality.

the creative firm of
Becker Design
Milwaukee, Wisconsin
with real-life designers
Neil Becker & Mary Eich
created this business card for
Eberhart Interiors

Coat of arms logo and aqua wash give an upscale representation of this interior design business.

the Townsend agency

3655 nobel drive | suite 470 | san diego, ca 92122

ken jacobs v.p. creative
KJCUPS@TOWNSENDAGENCY.COM

tel 619.457.4888 | ext 101 | fax 619.453.7010

the creative firm of
The Townsend Agency
San Diego, California
with real-life designer
Gail Look-Yan
created this business card for
The Townsend Agency

Business card with a plan was designed to also be used as a Rolodex card, making it convenient for the recipient to save contact information about the company.

MICHAEL WILSON

ARCHITECTURAL

PHOTOGRAPHY

MICHAEL WILSON

7015 SAN MATEO BLVD.

DALLAS, TEXAS 75223

TELEPHONE 214.328.8627

FACSLMILE 214.328.8627

the creative firm of
David Carter Design Assoc.
Dallas, Texas
with real-life designer
Randall Hill
created this business card for
Michael Wilson Architectural Photography

Examples of specialty photography are printed on one side of this business card. Large and tall size of card repeats the shape of much of the photographer's subjects.

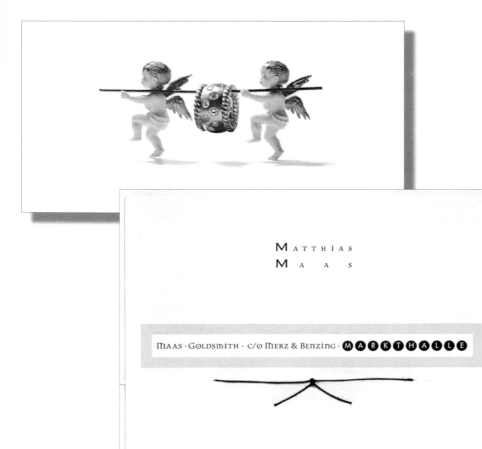

M ATTHIAS
M A A S

Maas · Goldsmith · c/o Merz & Benzing · MARKTHALLE

70173 Stuttgart · Tel.: 0711/246486 · Fax: 2367968

Öffnungszeiten

Montag   Donnerstag
        bis   und
Mittwoch   Freitag
9.30 - 18.30 Uhr   9.30 - 20.00 Uhr

Samstag
9.00 - 16.00 Uhr

the creative firm of
HEBE Werbung + Design
Leonberg, Germany
with real-life designer
Reiner Hebe
created this business card for
Zuwelier Maas

Hand stitched card is bound as a mini booklet.
Black-and-white photography showcases
goldsmith's work, while complementing necessary
business information.

the creative firm of
Triad, Inc.
Larkspur, California
with real-life designers
Michael Hinshaw, Michael Dambrowski,
& Diana Kollanyi
created these business cards for
Pacific Video Resources

Similar logos, with various background textures, all use the same color scheme. This instigates individuality (each cardholder has a different texture) while maintaining corporate identity.

JEFF PICCININI
Editor
Production Services

PACIFIC VIDEO RESOURCES

2331 Third Street
San Francisco CA 94107
415 864-5679
Voice Mail 205
Fax 415 864-2059
E-mail piccinini@pvr.com
www.pvr.com

JAN CROSBY
Technical Director
Strategic Partner

PACIFIC VIDEO RESOURCES

2331 Third Street
San Francisco CA 94107
415 864-5679
Voice Mail 213
Fax 415 864-2059
E-mail crosby@pvr.com
www.pvr.com

JOHN HORTON
Client Services

PACIFIC VIDEO RESOURCES

2331 Third Street
San Francisco CA 94107
415 864-5679
Voice Mail 214
Fax 415 864-2059
E-mail horton@pvr.com
www.pvr.com

PETE PENEBRE
Audio Engineer

PACIFIC VIDEO RESOURCES

2331 Third Street
San Francisco CA 94107
415 864-5679
Voice Mail 215
Fax 415 864-2059
E-mail penebre@pvr.com
www.pvr.com

T H A L L O N
A R C H I T E C T U R E

Dee Etzwiler

Designer

2303 McMorran Street
Eugene, OR 97403

Phone: 541.344.5210
Fax· 541.344.9868
E-mail: thallonarch@continet.com

the creative firm of
Funk & Associates
Eugene, Oregon
with real-life designers
Christopher Berner & Sandy Lui
created this business card for
Thallon Architecture

Negative space in sketchy logo forms the initial letter of this business.

real-life designer
Graham Allen
Richmond, Kentucky
created this business card for
Graham Allen

Unusually-sized card offers a full bleed, photographic metaphor for this design student's name. Back is printed with location information and black-and-white image as a border.

Graham Allen

•

graphic designer

212 College View Dr.
Richmond, KY
40475

•

606.623.6042

email: annagram@ix.netcom.com

the creative firm of
Kendra Power Design & Communication
Pittsburgh, Pennsylvania
with real-life designer
Larkin Werner
created this business card for
Kickapoo

Roughly-drawn illustrations, indicative of native American heritage, are used on the front of this card in black and green, and reversed out of full bleed green on the back.

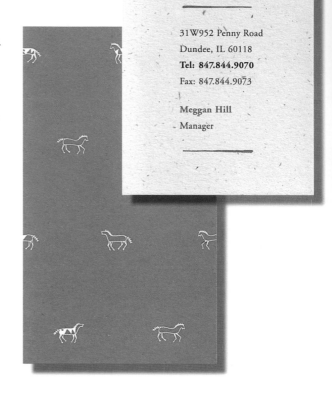

KICKAPOO

31W952 Penny Road
Dundee, IL 60118
Tel: 847.844.9070
Fax: 847.844.9073

Meggan Hill
Manager

real-life designer
Alfred Viola
Los Angeles, California
created this business card for
Donavan Freberg

Radioactive green emanates from the center of a classic microphone illustration. Radioman, Donavan Freberg, provides services "from concept to commercial."

Donavan Freberg
RADIOMAN

Tel: 310 473 9062
Fax: 310 473 9032

11033 Massachusetts Ave. #20
Los Angeles, California 90025

FROM CONCEPT TO COMMERCIAL

LAVERDONK

SUZANNE VAN CUYK

TRAINING
INSTRUCTION
SALES

LAVERDONK DRESSAGE

38 LIMEKILN ROAD
DOYLESTOWN, PA 18901
215-348-7848
215-348-3401 FAX

the creative firm of
Workhorse Design
Lehighton, Pennsylvania
with real-life designers
Constance Kovar & Anthony Taibi
created this business card for
Laverdonk Dressage

Silhouette of horse and rider walks out of negative into positive
space of logo. Partial logo is enlarged and screened in background.

the creative firm of
Paul Kaza Associates, Inc.
So. Burlington, Vermont
with real-life art director & designer
Karin T. Johnson
created this business card for
Oil 'n Go

Traffic light imagery printed in black and green is an excellent device
for this business. Wraparound type serves as a frame, repeating the
rounded corners of the card.

inspection • radiator flush & fill   **DAVID DRIVE**

SUSIE WILSON ROAD

17 pt. oil change, transmission fluid & air conditioning service • tune-up • sta/e

OIL
n
GO

ROB REMILLARD
manager
2 David Drive Essex Junction, VT 05452
PHONE | 879-2707
FAX | 879-2626

the creative firm of
Sagmeister Inc.
New York, New York
created this business card for
Boonshoft Vintage Rentals

Business in a very specialized field, vintage amplifier rentals, employs retro-style artwork to suggest a time frame relative to its merchandise.

the creative firm of
Cathey Associates
Dallas, Texas
with real-life designer
Matt Westapher
created this business card for
The University Club

Understated design integrates blind embossing with simple black printing.

b

Emanuel
Barbosa
Design

Rua da Vassada, 1682
Milheirós
4470 Maia
Tel. 02 - 9011868
Portugal

the creative firm of
Vestigio
Sra. Da Hora, Portugal
with real-life designer
Emanuel Barbosa
created this business card for
Emanuel Barbosa Design

Narrow card and lots of white space are apropos design elements
employed in the Minimalist approach to this card.

the creative firm of
Becker Design
Milwaukee, Wisconsin
with real-life designers
Neil Becker & Laura Manthey
created this business card for
Garbs

Freestyle calligraphy gives the impression that the clothes
and accessories sold at Garbs are casual, comfortable, fun.

garbs

clothing   accessories   jewelry

Cari Simon

Ruby Isle 2205 North Calhoun Road
Brookfield, Wisconsin 53005
Phone 414 780-0909 Fax 414 780-0910

the creative firm of
**Hornall Anderson
Design Works**
Seattle, Washington
with real-life designers
**Jack Anderson, Scott Eggers,
& Leo Raymundo**
created this business card for
Mahlum & Nordfors

Solid structure within a stroke of artistry describes the logo of the architectural firm originally known as Mahlum & Nordfors McKinley Gordon.

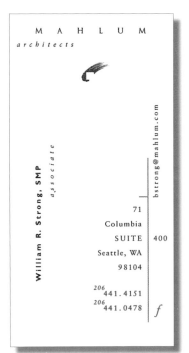

Amy Wong-Freeman
architect

**MAHLUM
&NORDFORS
McKINLEY
GORDON**

2505
Third Avenue
Suite 219
Seattle, WA
98121

206 441 4151
206 441 0478 F

architecture interiors planning

CONNECT

MAHLUM
architects

William R. Strong, SMP
associate

bstrong@mahlum.com

71
Columbia
SUITE 400
Seattle, WA
98104

206 441.4151
206 441.0478   f

the creative firm of
**Hornall Anderson
Design Works**
Seattle, Washington
with real-life designers
**Jack Anderson, Heidi Favour,
& Margaret Long**
created this business card for
Mahlum Architects

When an architectural firm (above) changed its name, this card was a result. Maintaining much of the original identity but with a newer look, the logo is used in the same manner; color and typography have evolved.

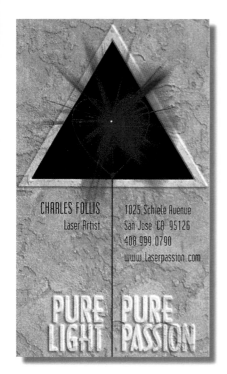

CHARLES FOLLIS
Laser Artist

1025 Schiele Avenue
San Jose CA 95126
408.999.0790
www.laserpassion.com

PURE LIGHT | PURE PASSION

the creative firm of
G.H. Bailey Company
San Jose, California
with real-life designer
Gwen Hagaman
created this business card for
Pure Light/Pure Passion

Red light streams from the center of a heart representing the business of this laser artist and the fire he feels for his work.

FOUR LEGS AND A TALE™
BY BOW MEOW INC.

the creative firm of
Phoenix Creative, St. Louis
St. Louis, Missouri
with real-life designer & illustrator
Deborah Finkelstein
created this business card for
Bow Meow, Inc.

Original text arrangement crowds words together but is not difficult to read. Dog pops up and cat drops in to peer at the viewer.

CARDS AND THE LIKE
FROM THE PET PSYCH™

PO BOX 148426
CHICAGO | ILLINOIS
60614

WORLD HQ 312.440.1658
FAX 312.440.9756

DEBORAH FINKELSTEIN

314.535.7955

CREATIVE DIRECTOR

the creative firm of
Sayles Graphic Design
Des Moines, Iowa
with real-life designer
John Sayles
created this business card for
Design Publications

Reminiscent of library index cards, tabs indicate that these samples of the publisher's work are but a few.

the creative firm of
Becker Design
Milwaukee, Wisconsin
created this business card for
Harry's Bar & Grill

Despite the fact this business card is for a perfectly respectable restaurant, by appearance of the card back it seems Harry's checkered past still follows him.

the creative firm of
Phoenix Creative, St. Louis
St. Louis, Missouri
with real-life designer
Ed Mantels-Seeker
created this business card for
Phoenix Creative

Reversed out of flame red, one side of card simply states the name
of the firm. The flip side has necessary information with tiny icons.

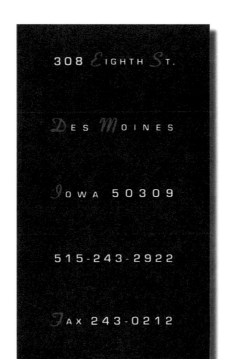

the creative firm of
Sayles Graphic Design
Des Moines, Iowa
created this business card for
Sayles Graphic Design

Shield of heavy lines is color foil
stamped on one side of card with
singular text of cardholder's name. Turn
card over for rest of info in the same
type treatment.

the creative firm of
Hoffmann & Angelic Design
Surrey (BC), Canada
with real-life designers
Andrea Hoffmann & Ivan Angelic
created this business card for
The Selling Edge

This card would be a good example to study in color composition class. Notice how the screened purple logo "changes" color when printed next to a darker color on the front, and against white on card back.

the creative firm of
Robert Meyers Communication Design & Planning
Pittsburgh, Pennsylvania
with real-life designer
Robert Meyers
created this business card for
Robert Meyers Communication Design & Planning

Straight and curved lines from logo can also be found in card edges. Excellent union of initials within logo keep each letter's identity while forming an entity.

Jane Brooke Mason

m

robert meyers
communication design
and planning

412 391 1150
412 391 1120 Facsimile
The Times Building, 336 Fourth Avenue
Pittsburgh, Pennsylvania 15222

LYNN MARTIN HASKIN, PH.D.

CHAIRMAN

**OLD
MARKET
STREET**

134 ARCH STREET

★

PHILADELPHIA, PA
19106

★

TELEPHONE
215·440·9166

FAX
215·440·0793

the creative firm of
Randi Wolf Design, Inc.
Glassboro, New Jersey
with real-life designer
Randi Wolf
created this business card for
Old Market Street

Illustrative art, symbolic of "Old Philadelphia" and wares sold on Old
Market Street, is incorporated into the logo of this organization that
promotes the redevelopment of Philadelphia's historic district.

the creative firm of
Cathey Associates, Inc.
Dallas, Texas
with real-life designer
Gordon Cathey
created this business card for
ERT1.com

Photos representative of the target audience are printed on
this Internet company's business card. Motto is reversed out of
full bleed purple on the back.

the creative firm of
Sayles Graphic Design
Des Moines, Iowa
created this business card for
Martin Crowder Salon

Business card doubles as an appointment card. Humorous illustration
immediately informs the viewer the cardholder is offering a hair cut.

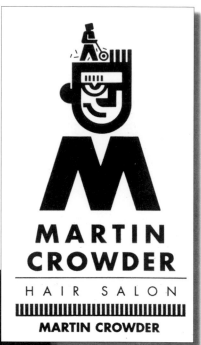

**MARTIN
CROWDER**

H A I R   S A L O N

MARTIN CROWDER

**5709 HICKMAN ROAD
DES MOINES, IOWA 50310**
IIIIIIIII **515-277-1709** IIIIIIIII

YOUR APPOINTMENT IS:

_____

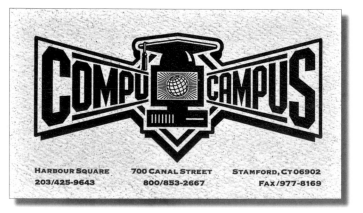

HARBOUR SQUARE   **700 CANAL STREET**   **STAMFORD, CT 06902**
203/425-9643   **800/853-2667**   **FAX/977-8169**

the creative firm of
Jack Tom Design
Monroe, Connecticut
with real-life designer
Jack Tom
created this business card for
Compu Campus

Logo that mimics the style of many traditional college crests
includes an almost iconic computer rendering to indicate the
nature of the Compu Campus business, computer distribution to
education.

Janet Payne
illustration

11 Mountain Church Road
Hopewell NJ 08525

phone 609·466·2436
fax 609·466·3640

the creative firm of
Janet Payne Graphic Designer
Hopewell, New Jersey
with real-life designer
Janet Payne
created this business card for
Janet Payne

Wonderful woodcut illustration serves as an example of this artist's work. Excellent choice of calligraphic font relates well with the drawing style presented.

the creative firm of
Phoenix Creative, St. Louis
St. Louis, Missouri
with real-life designer
Elizabeth Williams
created this business card for
moses.com

Circular theme in typography makes reference to the dot in "dot com". Hole is punched in business name to stand for the letter o. Thoughtful touch is a phonetic spelling of the cardholder's last name which surely alleviates any uneasiness about calling because of pronunciation mistake.

m○ses.com

DAN MAUZY (MŌ-ZAY) // *Chief Marketing Officer*

p. 314 236-2449 / *dmauzy@moses.com*
www.moses.com // 8000 Maryland Avenue / St. Louis, Missouri 63105

the creative firm of
DFacto
Balboa, California
created this business card for
Tina Casey Photography

Monochromatic, rather mysterious, photo showcases work of
photographer. Checkering of card stock shows through
printing in light areas.

TINA CASEY
PHOTOGRAPHY

714 • 675 • 2952
2008 BARRANCA
NEWPORT BEACH
CALIFORNIA 92660

Michael J. Goldblatt
President and
Chief Executive Officer

T / 978.851.8900 x 145
mgoldblatt@ibhome.com
F / 978.851.8901

INTELLIGENT BIOCIDES

200 Ames Pond Drive
Tewksbury, MA 01876.9998 USA
www.ibhome.com

the creative firm of
Phoenix Creative, St. Louis
St. Louis, Missouri
with real-life designer
Ed Mantels-Seeker
created this business card for
Intelligent Biocides

Technical-looking font was chosen for this company whose
business is antimicrobial products. Clean edges and the color,
silver, work well to suggest a futuristic quality.

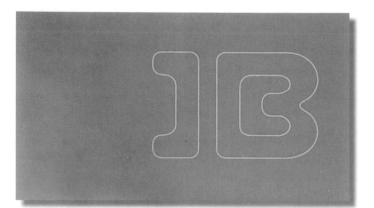

the creative firm of
Mires Design, Inc.
San Diego, California
created this business card for
Nextec

Embossed and printed logo is comprised of natural photographs out
of which is reversed the business name. The company manufactures
weather resistant fabric.

the creative firm of
Hornall Anderson Design Works
Seattle, Washington
created this business card for
Alta Beverage Company

Stylized letter A's in the company name began with a serif
font that was simplified, and to which a brush stroke was
added. Choice of blue is a strong indicator that this company
has something to do with water. In fact, they bottle it.

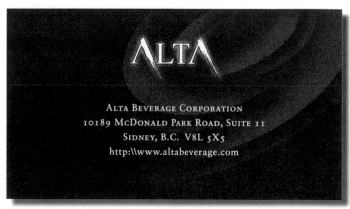

the creative firm of
Ellen Bruss Design
Denver, Colorado
with real-life art director
Ellen Bruss

and illustrator
G. Carr
plus designer
Jason C. Otero
created these cards for
Home on the Range

There is more to life
than increasing its speed.

Mahatma Gandhi

ELK BRIDGE CENTER
32214 ELLINGWOOD TRAIL
EVERGREEN CO 80439

PH 303 679 1111

Two sizes of folded cards serve as both business cards
and merchandise tags. Quotes on card insides and
screened illustrations on card backs are in keeping with
"Home on the Range" spirit.

Please, God, help me to be
the person that my dog thinks I am.

Anonymous

ELK BRIDGE CENTER
32214 ELLINGWOOD TRAIL
EVERGREEN CO 80439

PH 303 679 1111

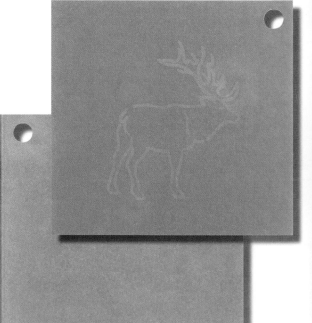

the creative firm of
Adkins/Balchunas
Providence, Rhode Island
created this business card for
Alfredo of Rome

Illustration by caricaturist, Al Hirschfeld, graces this business
card for an Italian restaurant. Several gradients add visual
interest, create focus, and ease the transition between
design elements.

the creative firm of
Adkins/Balchunas
Providence, Rhode Island
with real-life designer
Jerry Balchunas
created this business card for
Nino's

Nice dimensionality of overlapping letters is effected by
outlines and gradients. Except for the logo, all capitals are
used in the typography. A diamond dots the i in the logo and
is then repeated as bullets in the phone numbers.

the creative firm of
Vrontikis Design Office
Los Angeles, California
created this business card for
Jackson's

Extra-heavy stock makes this a very substantial card. Barbed wired treatment is subtly mimicked in logo.

the creative firm of
Hornall Anderson Design Works
Seattle, Washington
with real-life designers
Jack Anderson, Suzanne Haddon,
David Bates, Mary Hermes, Heidi Favour,
Mary Chin Hutchison, & Virginia Le
created this business card for
McCaw Corporation

Card for an international wireless communications company is printed in different languages on opposite sides.

STARR LITIGATION SERVICES, INC

1201 Grand Avenue
West Des Moines, IA 50265
starrlit@aol.com

KATHLEEN C. KAUFFMAN   (515) 224-1616 EXT. 135
Chief Executive Officer   Fax: (515) 224-4863

1201 Grand Avenue
West Des Moines, IA 50265
(515) 224-1616   Fax: (515) 224-4863

34522 N. Scottsdale Road, Suite D8
Scottsdale, AZ 85262
(602) 488-2750   Fax: (602) 488-4167

the creative firm of
Sayles Graphic Design
Des Moines, Iowa
with real-life designer
John Sayles
created this business card for
Starr Litigation

Horizontal lines, in the form of text or actual lines, abound on this horizontal business card. Back side of card is printed with three iconic images, which refer to the litigation process, within circles; curves are cut on the top corners of the card.

the creative firm of
Hornall Anderson Design Works
Seattle, Washington
with real-life designers
Jack Anderson & David Bates
created this business card for
Capons Rotisserie Chicken

Pinking at card top suggests the top of a brown bag. Color follows this theme reminding the customer that the restaurant also features takeout.

CAPONS
ROTISSERIE CHICKEN

Roger Hammerstrom
General Manager
Wallingford

1815
North 45th Street
Seattle, WA
98103

206 547-3949

the creative firm of
Scott Brown Design
Redwood City, California
with real-life designers
Laikit Chan & Scott Brown
created these business cards for
Scott Brown Design

Series of business cards uses the same color scheme on all cards. Type is treated similarly in the information sections. Artwork differs greatly from card to card displaying a variety of style from one firm.

DESIGNER
Scott Brown

STUDIO
650/261.9051
www.scottbrowndesign.com
designing daily at... 7 Cerrito Place
Redwood City California 94061 fax-650/261.9053
email-scottbdzin@batnet.com | ESTABLISHED 1992

STUDIO 650/261.9051 | www.scottbrowndesign.com
designing daily at... 7 Cerrito Place - Redwood City California 94061
fax-650/261.9053 *email-scottdzin@batnet.com* | ESTABLISHED 1992

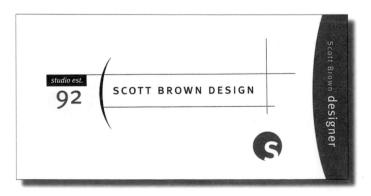

studio est.
92 | SCOTT BROWN DESIGN

Scott Brown **designer**

SCOTT BROWN

designer

SCOTT BROWN DESIGN

STUDIO 650/261.9051 | www.scottbrowndesign.com
designing daily at... 7 Cerrito Place - Redwood City California 94061
fax-650/261.9053 email-scottbdzin@batnet.com | ESTABLISHED 1992

the studio of
SCOTT BROWN
design

STUDIO 650/261.9051 | www.scottbrowndesign.com
designing daily at... 7 Cerrito Place - Redwood City California 94061
fax -650/261.9053 email-scottdzin@batnet.com | ESTABLISHED 1992

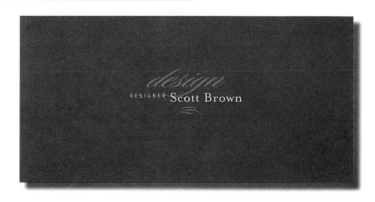

Graphic Design

Ron Crain
1970 Hillgate Way – D
Simi Valley, California 93065
805-526-1786 Fax 805-389-9569

the creative firm of
Crain Design Office
Simi Valley, California
created this business card for
Ron Crain

Simply-stated card offers a gracefully-abstract crane in reference
to the graphic designer's name.

the creative firm of
Sandy Gin Design
Palo Alto, California
with real-life designer
Sandy Gin
created this business card for
It's All Good

Upscale caterer's business card is adorned with illustrations of whole
foods and primitive figures indicating the cuisine is natural and fresh.

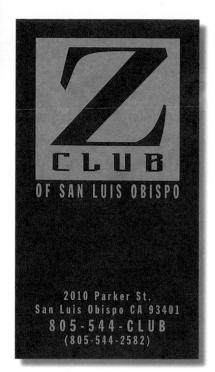

the creative firm of
Sandy Gin Design
Palo Alto, California
with real-life designer
Sandy Gin
created this business card for
Z Club

Though the majority of this nightclub's business card is black, it's black ink printed over brown stock. It's much easier to cover light with dark than the other way around.

the creative firm of
Phoenix Creative, St. Louis
St. Louis, Missouri
with real-life designer
Jenny Anderson
created this business card for
Vie

Printed with a smeared effect, this retail women's clothing card integrates grunge fonts with more traditional sans serif. Illustrative logo echoes the looseness of its surrounding elements.

the creative firm of
Gee + Chung Design
San Francisco, California
with real-life art director
Earl Gee
and designers
Earl Gee & Fani Chung
created this business card for
Frontline Now!

Part of company name, "Now!", is shadowed in the background slightly larger in size than the remaining name. Interesting mix of font sizes on card back achieve focus.

FRONTLINE **NOW!**

HIGH TECHNOLOGY'S CHANNEL SALES & MARKETING FORCE

FRONTLINE NOW!

Jan Soulé
VICE PRESIDENT OF MARKETING

EMAIL
JSOULE@FRONTLINENOW.COM

DIRECT TEL
408.431.1816

100 BORLAND WAY
SCOTTS VALLEY CA 95066-3249

TEL
408.395.4ROI

FAX
408.431.1829

WEB
WWW.FRONTLINENOW.COM

the creative firm of
Rauscher Design, Incorporated
Louisville, Kentucky
with real-life designers
Janet Rauscher & Susan Morganti
created this business card for
Ditto Sales, Inc.

Curved die cut on card edge is employed as missing letters in the business name. On the front, it serves as the capital D, the back uses it for the letter o.

Ditto Sales Inc.

Gene Hostetter
Sales Manager

P.O. Box **850**
Jasper, IN
47547-0850

www.dittosales.com

812

482.3043 *Telephone*
482.9318 *Facsimile*

the creative firm of
Vestigio
Sra. Da Hora, Portugal
with real-life designer
Emanuel Barbosa
created this business card for
José Pinho

Capital J intertwines through the P, both initials of the jeweler to
whom this card belongs. Back is printed full bleed with bittersweet
orange.

real-life designer
Michael Lancashke
Portland, Oregon
created this business card for
Damian Conrad Photography

Business cards are printed in one color, gray. A separate four-color
printing yields various Polaroid-style photos that are trimmed out
and applied to the cards.

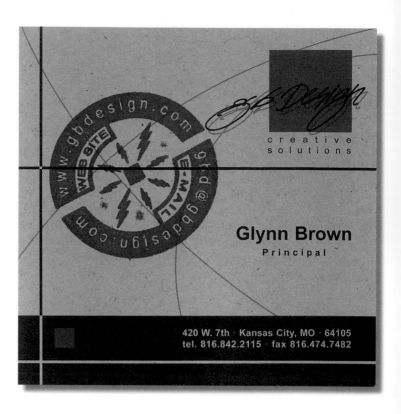

the creative firm of
gb Design, Inc.
Kansas City, Missouri
with real-life designers
Glynn Brown, Ryan Lorei,
Joseph Stramberg, & Jill Bergthold
created this business card for
gb Design, Inc.

Large, square card printed on heavy card stock is sure to be remembered. Back lists the design services offered.

CHIP SIMONS | PHOTOGRAPHY

CHIP SIMONS
PHOTOGRAPHER

1570 WEST BOSQUE LOOP
BOSQUE FARMS, NM 87068-9072
TELEPHONE: [505]869.0344
FACSIMILE: [505]869.0944
EMAIL: CHIPSHOT@RT66.COM
INTERNET: WWW.CHIPSIMONS.COM

the creative firm of
Strong Productions
Cedar Rapids, Iowa
with real-life designers
Todd Schatzberg, Matt Doty, & Brian Cox
created this business card for
Chip Simons Photography

Photographer's business card is die cut and printed along top edge
to resemble a negative strip.

Stacey Dawrant's Nutritional Concepts

4431 INDEPENDENCE TRAIL
EVERGREEN, CO 80439
(303) 670-1621

the creative firm of
VSA Partners
Chicago, Illinois
with real-life designer
Bob Domenz
created this business card for
Stacey Dawrant Nutritional Concepts

Humorous business card for a professional nutritionist
reads as nutritional facts/ingredients section of
packaged food.

Nutritional Facts

Serving Size: 1 Professional
Suggested Servings: As needed

Amount per serving	% Daily Value with Stacey
Improved Lifestyle	110%
Entertaining Information	118%
Useful Food Facts	114%
Professional Advice	155%
Better Health	190%

% Daily Value calculated by average reader benefit

INGREDIENTS: MASTERS DEGREE IN HUMAN NUTRITION, REGISTERED DIETITIAN, PUBLISHED WRITER, MEMBER ADA, COLLEGE INSTRUCTOR, PROFESSIONAL SPEECH DELIVERY, SALUBRIOUS PERSPECTIVE, HUMOROUS, WITTY, NO PRESERVATIVES OR ARTIFICIAL FLAVORS.

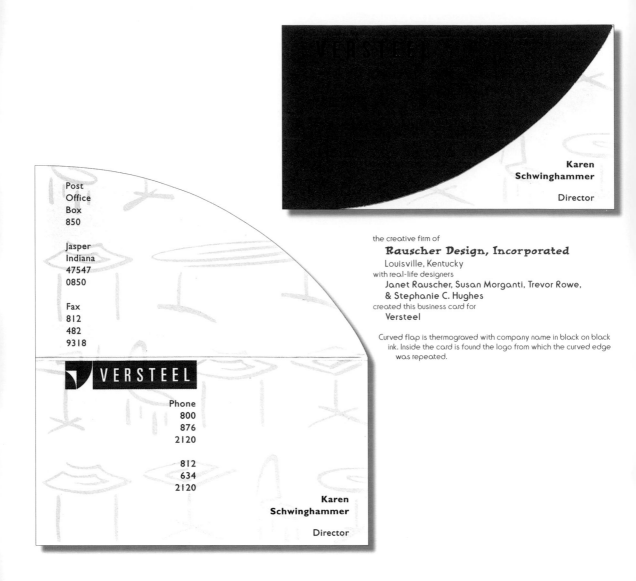

**Karen
Schwinghammer**

Director

Post
Office
Box
850

Jasper
Indiana
47547
0850

Fax
812
482
9318

VERSTEEL

Phone
800
876
2120

812
634
2120

**Karen
Schwinghammer**

Director

the creative firm of
Rauscher Design, Incorporated
Louisville, Kentucky
with real-life designers
Janet Rauscher, Susan Morganti, Trevor Rowe,
& Stephanie C. Hughes
created this business card for
Versteel

Curved flap is thermograved with company name in black on black
ink. Inside the card is found the logo from which the curved edge
was repeated.

InterVector

Intervector, Comércio Internacional, Lda.
Rua da Misericórdia, 16, 3º andar
Tels. +351. (0)53. 619203/619855
Fax +351. (0)53. 611872
P-4710 Braga Portugal

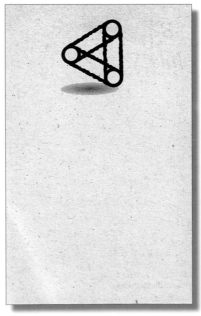

the creative firm of
Vestigio
Sra. Da Hora, Portugal
with real-life designer
Emanuel Barbosa
created this business card for
Intervector

Importer/exporter's logo is three points
interconnected, forming a triangle. It's
slightly askew indicating forward
movement.

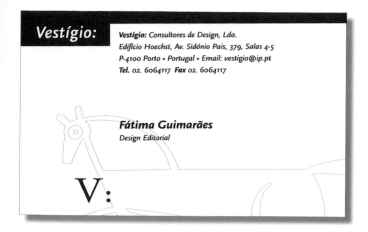

the creative firm of
Vestigio
Sra. Da Hora, Portugal
with real-life designer
Emanuel Barbosa
created this business card for
Vestigio

Design consultancy's logo is a linear illustration of a horse. It's printed
in part, with a two-sided bleed on the business card.

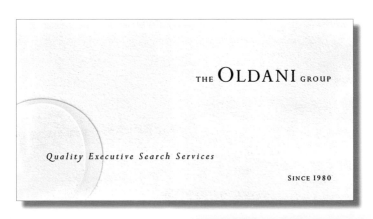

the creative firm of
GA Design
Bellevue, Washington
with real-life designer
Kurt Niedermeier
created this business card for
The Oldani Group

Card with basic information achieves an elegant image with
the use of a blurred Corinthian column printed in the background on one side. Partial company initial is embossed in
bottom corner.

167

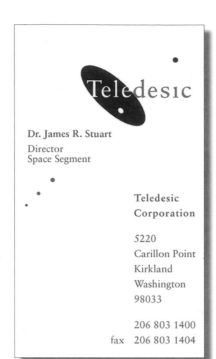

Teledesic

Dr. James R. Stuart
Director
Space Segment

Teledesic
Corporation

5220
Carillon Point
Kirkland
Washington
98033

206 803 1400
fax   206 803 1404

CASTILE
VENTURES

Nina F. Saberi
GENERAL PARTNER
nina@castileventures.com

890 Winter Street

SUITE 140
Waltham, MA 0 2 4 5 1

TEL 781.890.0060
FAX 781.890.0065

www.castileventures.com

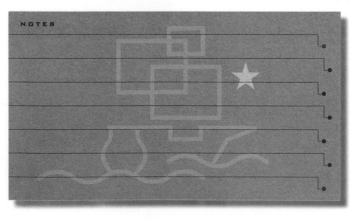

NOTES

Altamiro Machado
Gestor de Projectos

Estudos de
Desenvolvimento
Económico e Social, Lda.

Av. Central, 45
Tel. 053. 616510/906
Fax 053. 611872
4710 Braga
Portugal

the creative firm of
Vestigio
Sra. Da Hora, Portugal
with real-life designer
Emanuel Barbosa
created this business card for
Vector XXI

Mixed fonts and alternative plays on positive and negative space
make an active-looking logo.

the creative firm of
CUBE Advertising & Design
St. Louis, Missouri
with real-life designers
David Chiow, Matt Marino
created this business card for
Northstar Management Co. LLC

Tiny North Star is die cut from a constellation map background.

KENNETH N. CATES
EXECUTIVE VICE PRESIDENT
10795 WATSON ROAD
ST. LOUIS, MISSOURI 63127
KCATES@NORTHSTARMGMT.COM

NORTHSTAR MANAGEMENT CO. LLC

314 821-3325 OFFICE
314 821-3988 FAX
314 974-6417 MOBILE
618 677-0243 HOME
314 491-7925 PAGER

the creative firm of
Hansen Design Company
Seattle, Washington
with real-life designers
Pat Hansen, Kate Dodd, Carrie Adams,
& Dominic Dunbar
created these business cards for
Hansen Design Company

Hansen employs the use of dots in varying sizes and colors all over their business cards. The letters in the company name are composed of small black dots. Mimicking this theme, larger modelled dots are staggered to create a visual texture which is then applied full bleed on card back and in a border on the card front.

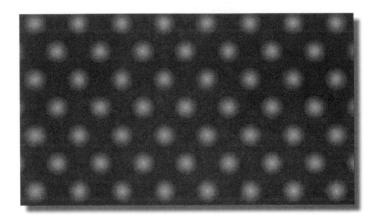

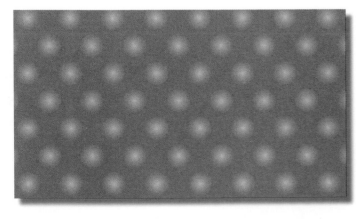

the creative firm of
Art's Image Creative Group Inc.
Oklahoma City, Oklahoma
with real-life designers
Fred Welch & Bridgett Minz
created this business card for
Art's Image Creative Group Inc.

Unique card stock is a striped, heavy vellum with almost a plastic feel. Logo is blind embossed, but printed with a gray "wash" to highlight dimensionality.

the creative firm of
Unicom
Milwaukee, Wisconsin
with real-life designers
Unicom
created this business card for
Ken Eichenbaum

This design firm developed a phonetic rebus for a client with a last name that might be confusing to pronounce.

the creative firm of
Phoenix Creative, St. Louis
St. Louis, Missouri
with real-life designer
Deborah Finkelstein
created this business card for
New World Post Productions

Tag-style business card is printed, scored, folded, and then punched with an eyelet.

the creative firm of
Fuse, Inc.
Laguna Beach, California
with real-life designer
Russell Pierce
created this business card for
Fuse, Inc.

Bold design is expressed in dark colors, and clean straight and curved lines. Logo is very substantial depicted in marble and other dimensional effects.

the creative firm of
Gee + Chung Design
San Francisco, California
with real-life art directors & designers
Earl Gee & Fani Chung
created this business card for
Berman Marketing Reserve

No one will forget this card. Printed front, back, and inside, metallic inks are used in accordance with dark purple. Extra touches on this folded card include edge die cuts, see-through die cut, and embossing—nice.

Meredith Robinson
technology marketing consultant

15127 NE 24th Street
Suite 466
Redmond, WA 98052

tel **206.369.3274**
fax 425.881.3959
meredith@mcrew.com

the creative firm of
Belyea
Seattle, Washington
with real-life art director
Patricia Belyea
and designer
Naomi Murphy
created these business cards for
Meredith & Crew

Each of these cards was printed with a slightly different clientele in mind as the job titles will attest. Printing in different colors makes it easier for the cardholder to grab the appropriate card without having to stop and read the fine print.

Meredith Robinson
principal

15127 NE 24th Street
Suite 466
Redmond, WA 98052

tel **206.369.3274**
fax 425.881.3959
meredith@mcrew.com

Meredith Robinson
columnist/writer

15127 NE 24th Street
Suite 466
Redmond, WA 98052

tel **206.369.3274**
fax 425.881.3959
meredith@mcrew.com

Meredith Robinson
designer

15127 NE 24th Street
Suite 466
Redmond, WA 98052

tel **206.369.3274**
fax 425.881.3959
meredith@mcrew.com

the creative firm of
Balderman Creative Services
San Juan Capistrano, California
with real-life designer
Barbara Balderman
created this business card for
Balderman Creative Services

Interesting mix of gradients and flat colors, and perfect and odd angles abound on this card. It all works together to create a lively unity.

the creative firm of
Hornall Anderson Design Works
Seattle, Washington
with real-life designers
Jack Anderson, Lisa Cerveny,
& Suzanne Haddon
created this business card for
Jamba Juice

Fibered card stock offers the same colors as those found in the printing. Card back is printed full bleed out of which a cornucopia of natural foods is reversed.

digital imaging group

the creative firm of
Cooksherman
San Francisco, California
with real-life designers
Ken Cook & I-Hua Chen
created this business card for
Digital Imaging Group

Curved die cut creates a unique edge on folded card when closed. Open the card for vitals.

Robert Aronoff
President & Executive Director

Post Office Box 6003	Pho 650.697.8722
Millbrae CA 94030	Fax 650.697.8726
	Pgr 415.254.3382

aronoffr@digitalimaging.org

digital imaging group

working together to build the future of imaging

JEFFREY G. SALTER
GENERAL MANAGER

JSALTER@NANOCOSM.COM

NANOCOSM TECHNOLOGIES, INC.
1291 E. HILLSDALE BLVD., SUITE 210
FOSTER CITY, CA 94404
TEL: 650.345.7400 | FAX: 650.345.7497

WWW.NANOCOSM.COM

the creative firm of
Gee + Chung Design
San Francisco, California
with real-life art director
Earl Gee
and designers
Earl Gee & Fani Chung
created this business card for
Nanocosm Technologies, Inc.

Gradient of black and fluorescent red creates the image of light. Used in the logo, it's repeated full bleed on card back with information reversed out of it.

NANOCOSM
TECHNOLOGIES, INC.

the creative firm of
Sayles Graphic Design
Des Moines, Iowa
with real-life designer
John Sayles
created this business card for
Casa Bonita

Furniture store has Southwestern motif within its logo. Theme is
continued in business card art.

the creative firm of
Becker Design
Milwaukee, Wisconsin
with real-life designer
Neil Becker
created this business card for
Zoom Messenger

Curves and sharp angles indicate speed and movement for the logo
of this messenger service. Complementing the treatment is a
brightly-colored gradient within the logo and printed full bleed on
the back.

225 East St. Paul Ave.
Suite 203
P.O. Box 1834
Milwaukee, WI 53201
Phone 414 289 9999
Fax 414 289 8388

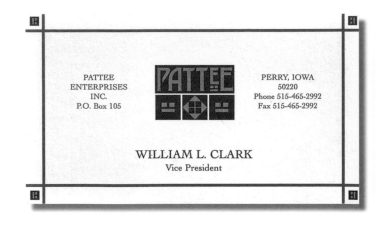

PATTEE
ENTERPRISES
INC.
P.O. Box 105

PERRY, IOWA
50220
Phone 515-465-2992
Fax 515-465-2992

WILLIAM L. CLARK
Vice President

the creative firm of
Sayles Graphic Design
Des Moines, Iowa
with real-life designer
John Sayles
created this business card for
Pattee Enterprises

All cards on this spread are for closely related, but individual companies. Each card plainly maintains the over-all identity yet has its own specificity. This one, for the owner of a hotel, employs a full bleed photo on the card back.

JANET R. LUETT
Director of Sales

the creative firm of
Sayles Graphic Design
Des Moines, Iowa
with real-life designer
John Sayles
created this business card for
Hotel Pattee

Business card for the hotel itself is a more encompassing design than the others. Elements originating here can be found on associated cards.

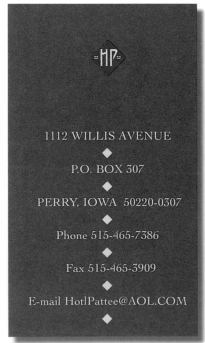

1112 WILLIS AVENUE

◆

P.O. BOX 307

◆

PERRY, IOWA 50220-0307

◆

Phone 515-465-7386

◆

Fax 515-465-3909

◆

E-mail HotlPattee@AOL.COM

◆

the creative firm of
Sayles Graphic Design
Des Moines, Iowa
with real-life designer
John Sayles
created this business card for
Hotel Pattee David's Milwaukee Diner

Card for diner located within Hotel Pattee serves as a dual card, highlighting either business on respective sides. Notice how the diner uses the same typographical style in its logo, but italicized.

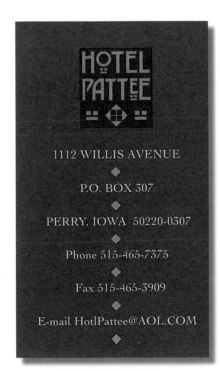

the creative firm of
Gryphon Art Studio
Prospect, Kentucky
with real-life designer
Elizabeth Perry Spalding
created this business card for
Professional Packaging

Clever card for a packaging company comes shrink wrapped!

Douglas P. Tennant
President

Post Office Box 17265
Louisville, Kentucky 40217

502-636-0262 tel

1-888-PRO-PACK

We have your

packaging needs

under wraps.

SUSAN A. MacLAUGHLIN

voice
(510) 845-0384

email
SusanM@MacLaughlinGroup.com

fax
(510) 845-0385

1922 M.L. King Jr. Way
Berkeley, California
94704-1016

the creative firm of
Fifth Street Design
Berkeley, California
with real-life partners
J. Clifton Meek & Brenton Beck
created this business card for
The MacLaughlin Group

Celtic knots were chosen as artwork for a card whose holder's name
has the same derivation.

the creative firm of
McGaughy Design
Falls Church, Virginia
with real-life designer
Malcolm McGaughy
created this business card for
McGaughy Design

These great temporary cards announced the design firm's
renovation. They were hand cut, hand stamped, and (give the
indication) probably thrown at clients amidst the mess and
furor.

the creative firm of
Design Guys
Minneapolis, Minnesota
with real-life designer
Mitch Morse
created this business card for
Hest & Kramer

Peel-off sticker doubles as a business card with location information on backing.

Steve Kramer

Hest & Kramer 5250 West 74th St. Edina, Mn. 55439
Tel: 612.831.3266 Fax: 612.831.4105 Chicago: 312.587.9741

the creative firm of
Boldface Design
Los Angeles, California
with real-life designers
Kevin Hummer & Susan Weber
created this business card for
Upper Cuts

Business/appointment card for a sports barbershop is strictly masculine in theme: bigger-than-typical, firmer-than-usual, with stronger-than-ordinary art.

YOUR NEXT APPOINTMENT IS

DATE   TIME

YOUR BARBER WILL BE

the creative firm of
A-Hill Design
Albuquerque, New Mexico
with real-life designers
Sandy Hill, Emma Roberts
created this business card for
Tech 2 Me

Communication is the message with pixellated, embossed lips
highlighted by outward arrows.

the creative firm of
Sayles Graphic Design
Des Moines, Iowa
with real-life designer
John Sayles
created this business card for
Big Daddy Photography

Sturdy stock is die cut in the shape of a camera for this
photography studio's business card.

Index